# Theatre for Conflict Resolution

# Theatre for Conflict Resolution
## In the Classroom and Beyond

Patricia Sternberg

HEINEMANN
Portsmouth, NH

**Heinemann**
A division of Reed Elsevier Inc.
361 Hanover Street
Portsmouth, NH 03801–3912
http://www.heinemann.com

*Offices and agents throughout the world*

**Library of Congress Cataloging-in-Publication Data**
Sternberg, Patricia.
    Theatre for conflict resolution: In the classroom and beyond / Patricia Sternberg.
        p.      cm.
    Includes bibliographical references
    ISBN 0–325–00088–3 (alk. paper)
    1. School violence—United States—Prevention.    2. Conflict management—United States.    3. Psychodrama—United States.
    4. Classroom management—United States.      I. Title.
    LB3013.3.S748    1998
    371.7'82—dc21                                                                        98–29706
                                                                                                CIP

Editor: Lisa A. Barnett
Production: Vicki Kasabian
Cover design: Jenny Jensen Greenleaf
Manufacturing: Courtney Ordway

Printed in the United States of America on acid-free paper
02  01  00          EB      2    3    4    5

This book is dedicated to all those who live, love, and practice drama and theatre as art and/or therapy.

# Contents

# Foreword

As I review the extraordinary growth of our field over the years in which I have been active in it, I am particularly conscious of the strides made both in drama therapy and in the use of drama and theatre in education. A text on conflict resolution for the teacher is therefore welcome for its contribution to the growing body of literature and for numerous other reasons. First among them is the book's timeliness. From difficulties in our human relationships to world conflicts it would seem that in these final years of the twentieth century we are all desperately seeking ways to defuse emotions and deal with problems without resorting to violence. Professor Sternberg has given us not only the means to reach these goals but also the tools for implementation. No less important than timeliness is the practicality of the text. Activities and exercises abound, all set in situations with which young people can identify and written in language they can understand.

The diversity of our society today is an area that we have only recently recognized as a source of conflict as well as riches. But in order to enjoy this rich body of material that the immigrants have brought us, we must face the problems that are the result of fear, ignorance, prejudice, anger, and violence. Professor Sternberg, in presenting conflicts on both individual and group levels, has faced the problems and included situations that the therapist and drama teacher can use.

Finally, and again of equal importance, is the balance maintained between the academic and the practical. The college student with little or no background in drama therapy will find the text accessible, whereas the more experienced or graduate student will discover something new in every chapter. Sternberg's expertise is well supported by her references and bibliographical material.

After a brief discussion of conflict, she suggests warm-ups and theatre games to promote cooperation and solidify a group. Exercises, mime and improvisation, monologues, point of view scenes, word plays, and short plays to act and complete are among the assignments for classroom and workshop leaders. Written in an easy style, the text leads the reader from simple and obvious conflicts to the more complex and subtle. Universal as the text is in scope, it is current in approach, and highly recommended to both drama teachers and drama therapists, for it will be useful to both.

Nellie McCaslin, Ph.D.
New York University

# Acknowledgments

Many thanks go to all the teachers who tested the materials in this book, the students who offered feedback, colleagues who gave suggestions, clients past and present who inspired me to explore new ways to resolve conflicts, and friends whose support made all things possible, including this book. I am also grateful to those peers who inspired me along my journey, beginning with Julie Thompson, who opened the door to drama and theatre for me, and to Vera Roberts, who gave me the opportunity to fly with it. In addition, I am deeply appreciative to all those who have gone before me in the many areas of drama and theatre and to those who have added to our knowledge of drama as therapy. I would especially like to thank the following people for their assistance above and beyond: Richard Sternberg and Dolly Beechman Schnall, my first readers always; Lisa Barnett for her belief in the work; Nina Garcia and Linda Cook for their support; and Janet Chenery for her counsel.

I would also like to thank the following teachers for their assistance, which included testing some of the materials in the book: Barry Cohen, Chris Colt, Ingrid Constantine, Linda Nelson, Susan Silverstein. Finally, I extend my thanks to all those students who offered feedback about the activities.

# Introduction

All the world's a stage
And all the men and women merely players;
They have their exits and their entrances,
And one man in his time plays many parts . . .

*Shakespeare*

Adolescents play many roles in life, and often the part they play is not one they choose or even like. It is thrust upon them by their peers, their parents, or their own imagined inadequacies coupled with low self-esteem. The roles selected by teenagers depend on where they are and who they are with. Most stances are familiar, such as "the tough guy," "the know-it-all," or "the I-couldn't-care-less—this-is-so-boring!" Some prefer celebrity roles like the latest rock stars or athletes. Madonna changed the "in" look with bright red lipstick. Adolescents play one role at home, another at school, and still a separate one with their friends. Another part they would like to play is usually lurking somewhere just below the surface in their fantasy lives.

The trouble with many of these roles, or parts adolescents play, is that they may bring about untimely exits. Unfortunately, these kinds of exits are not onstage but from real life. The varying kinds of violence seen on film, TV, or the stage are deceptively simple. The victim gets up and walks away when the scene is over, but the violence occurring in the lives of our adolescents is lethal and permanent. Unfortunately, violent crime committed by and against young people is on the rise and getting worse all the time.

In 1993 the National Education Association reported that on a daily basis 100,000 students carried guns to school, 160,000 missed classes for fear of physical harm, and 40 were injured or killed by firearms. In New York City the leading cause of death for adolescents is homicide. In California more kids die from gun violence than car crashes.

In his first inaugural address President Clinton said of our young people, "They see so little. They have no imagination." Adolescents involved in violence never have a chance to see the world as it is. They see it as a place with no future, possibilities, or hope, and it makes them angry—at the world, at adults, and at those they consider responsible. They feel alone and fear tomorrow. They slap on the Walkman and escape to a world of rage and isolation. They close their eyes to anything new and anyone unfamiliar or different regardless of their own ethnic origin or racial heritage. They disconnect from the world.

These are the problems that face us all today, especially those of us who are educators trying to deal with this population. The problems are all too evident. How can we reach these teenagers? What can we do to connect with them? How do we open their eyes and ears so that we can take them someplace else, show them other possibilities in their lives? We need to help them reconnect to the world. Drama and theatre connect people and ideas.

Schools around the country are scurrying to find new approaches to deal with violence. Educators are trying out programs in conflict resolution, problem solving, peer mediation, and even ways to teach moral reasoning and ethical action. With all our technology and instant international communication, e-mail and the Internet, many young people still know only their immediate surroundings and the people in them. For too many, their neighborhood or street corner defines the boundaries of their existence. Everything else on the outside is unknown, foreign, unsafe, to be avoided. Just as their world has shrunk, so have opportunities for understanding, learning, and discovering who they are or can be.

How can we help our young people acquire the skills to move beyond their narrow worlds, to discover new places and experiences, to forge meaningful relationships, to make sense and order out of the world as it exists? What are some of the positive roles young people can learn to play? What are the skills adolescents need to see beyond today, to dream of a better tomorrow, to develop their inner resources to imagine what could be? How do we stimulate their curiosity to explore their beliefs and their courage to stand up for their convictions and make their voices heard? There is a way, a way that works. That way is through the theatre and drama.

The terms *drama* and *theatre* in this book are used to designate two different forms. *Drama* (as in *creative drama*) refers to the process that includes a variety of techniques such as improvisation, role play, play making, and theatre games, while the term *theatre* is used to describe a product, a performance in front of an audience. The theatre experience includes a script, director, and actors who work to create an agreed-upon aesthetic for the performance. In addition, theatre calls for a performance space and an audience, while drama can be done anywhere and by anyone regardless of the functional level of the individuals.

Theatre has always been a mirror of our society. In our dramatic literature we examine all of life's problems. Drama educators and theatre practitioners know about reaching young people through the theatre. We can show them a multicultural world and help them understand others when they try on the role of someone different from themselves. In the theatre they can go to a hundred different places and play as many different roles where they can safely explore all sorts of possibilities. This theatre experience does not have to occur in a special building, on a formal stage, or even a raised platform. Theatre can take place anywhere from a grassy knoll to a garage or basement. The place is secondary to the experience. The theatre offers a symbolic safe place, a nonjudgmental environment, and an aesthetic distance for exploring any of life's problems or conflicts.

In theatre, youngsters learn various life skills through collaboration rather than confrontation. Theatre is an ideal medium for learning how to cooperate, for finding alternatives to violence, for broadening the individual's world, and for understanding ourselves and others. Studies done by the American Alliance for Theatre and Education show that the theatre experience teaches discipline and cooperation, enhances listening skills, promotes concentration, and provides a feeling of success as part of a team. It enhances the ability to verbalize feelings, including acceptable ways of dealing with anger, frustration, jealousy, joy, sex, or love.

The theatre demands cooperation, which promotes better impulse control and positive peer relationships. It encourages self-esteem and promotes problem-solving skills. Conflict is no stranger to theatre; drama is built on the premise of conflict. What could be a more natural resource with which to explore conflict resolution?

People respond to conflict in a variety of ways, beginning with the old adage, "fight or flight." Indeed these are the most common responses to conflict: confrontation or avoidance. However, there is a third response, which theatre promotes: *collaboration through communication.* Communication is a two-way street. Playing a role entails not only verbal skills and body language but also active listening.

The theatre, then, is a place that can enlarge a young person's world, as well as his or her understanding of that world and the people in it. The experience can bring about an awakening of the self. Participants can play a variety of roles, interpret every emotion known to man, rant and rave, cry and scream—all in a safe environment without having to worry about real guns or knives. It is a place to try out new behaviors, to play new roles or old roles in different ways, without fear of consequences.

When you play the role of someone different from yourself, you often make discoveries about who you really are, rather than the person you think you should be or others tell you to be. The theatre offers enough distance, a symbolic safe place, to explore the conflicts human beings have shared since time began. This distancing can go a long way toward giving young people room to experiment and discover new ways in which to deal with their own problems. Their experiences can be felt and shared.

Drama serves as a means to revitalize young people. It can be that bridge to reconnect our adolescents to the possibilities that life has to offer. The distancing through literature of enactment gives them a safe armor in which to talk about issues without being too vulnerable. When we play the part of a character different from ourselves, we learn something about that person and his or her differences. With that knowledge, we often come to understand something new about ourselves as well.

The activities in this book are presented in progressive order, chapter by chapter, so that even the uninitiated can begin to work with drama. The text begins with simple drama activities and moves forward to the more complicated aspects of creating theatre. It is not only for those teachers who already know the power of drama, but also for those educators, adolescent group workers, recreation leaders, and parents who want to learn more. This book will give you the opportunity to help broaden adolescents' worlds, to open their eyes to the possibilities in life, and to help them acquire skills for making those possibilities become reality. The book will help you guide young people through conflict and resolution, through failure to success, from a limited world to an unlimited one. Trust yourself and the work, and there are no limits to what you can do through theatre. Break a leg!

# 1

# What Is Conflict?

Let us never negotiate out of fear. But let us never fear
to negotiate.

*John F. Kennedy*

## FLIGHT OR FIGHT

Drama is based on conflict. The very essence of the theatre is
conflict: man against nature, man against man, and man against
himself. Every drama can be placed in one of these categories.
Conflict is a natural part of life. Without conflict there probably
would be no personal growth in individuals or changes in society.
Actually, life would be pretty dull without conflict. It is not conflict
that presents problems, but how we deal with that conflict. What
could be more natural than to learn how to resolve conflict through
drama and theatre techniques? All conflicts derive from a threat or
challenge to ego or respect, or from rekindling of past grievances.

When we resolve a conflict to our satisfaction, we feel a sense of
success and satisfaction. Likewise, when we let that conflict get the
better of us, we feel a sense of failure or even guilt, especially if we
resorted to violence. Either way, we can learn from that conflict, and
it can have beneficial results. Learning how to deal with anger is part
of growing up, of becoming mature, no matter what our chrono-
logical age. What we too often do not learn in our schools, homes,
or societies are ways to deal successfully with conflict. Through the
process of drama and the product of theatre we can practice critical

1

thinking, problem solving, conflict resolution, and skill building to resolve conflicts creatively without resorting to violence.

## DEFINITIONS

What is conflict? Dictionaries give us a variety of definitions: "to come into collision or disagreement, be contradictory, at variance, or in opposition; clash," "to do battle or struggle," "a controversy; a quarrel." Simply put, conflict occurs when one person wants one thing and the other person wants another, or when two people want the same object, and there is only one of those objects available. That is the basis for conflict and for drama. How many plays have been written about two men wanting the same woman or two women in love with the same man? If the two share mutual respect, the conflict usually resolves nonviolently. However, if the two people in love with the same woman are enemies or strangers, violent conflict often erupts, especially if ego is involved, as it usually is. From that basic conflict comes the collision, quarrel, or battle.

## INSIDE CONFLICTS

Conflict comes from two directions: both *inside* and *outside*. The conflict we feel within ourselves is the inside conflict (people against themselves). "I want to go there, but I know I shouldn't," or "I don't want to do that, but I know I should." We are all faced with internal conflicts every day of our lives. These simple conflicts require choices. "I want to go to the concert tonight, but I promised I would visit my great-aunt Lulu." This conflict requires problem solving. If we have learned to delay gratification and to practice problem-solving skills, we have no difficulty making the decision that is right for us at the moment. However, if we have had no experience in delayed gratification or problem solving, our personal conflicts are governed by the need for immediate pleasure. The need for instant gratification says we know only one way to resolve conflicts. The art of resolving them successfully is yet to be learned.

## OUTSIDE CONFLICTS

Although some inside conflicts prove difficult, the majority of our problems occur when the conflict comes from outside. Resolving conflicts with others requires understanding, negotiation, or compromise—sometimes all three. Conflicts that occur among young people typically fall into four categories:

1. Raunchy rumors
2. Noxious names
3. Fractured friendships
4. Terroristic threats

Many of us have been the victim of a raunchy rumor at one time or another. "Robert said you were doing pot in the bathroom with your head in the toilet." Or "Myra said you were driving drunk in your underwear last night." These kinds of statements usually make you angry even before you have a chance to check out the source. Maybe it wasn't Robert who started the rumor but somebody else entirely different. However, by the time you see Robert, you're probably ready to pop him whether he was the one who started the rumor or not.

Noxious names or name-calling is right up there on the list as a top conflict launcher. Back in the sixties, a classic put-down or put-on (take your choice) was "Your mother wears Army boots." That line probably wouldn't bother anybody today. Everybody wears boots these days, men and women. So what constitutes name-calling can change over the years. Today you'd probably hear "You're a ho" (the euphemism for whore) or "You're a wuz" (a nerd or nothing), not to mention some of the more picturesque terms describing body parts. These derogatory labels seem to be passed down from one generation to the next with their own subtle or not-so-subtle variations.

When friendships break up, both participants may consider themselves the injured party and feel victimized by the fractured friendship. Conflicts are ripe for bursting forth at this point, especially if secrets or intimate details were shared during the friendship and are now public information. The "get even" syndrome sets in, and the two parties are off and running with their private vendettas. Conflict can occur on sight with no discussion, information, or mediation likely.

Of course, the classic conflict occurs with the terroristic threat. In this situation the majority of us revert to the classic human reaction: fight or flight. These threats take place on a variety of levels. When someone says, "Stand up and fight," you have a clear-cut choice: to fight or to run away! But when someone says, "If you don't stay away from my girl, I'll kill you," it could be an idle threat or a very real one. The time, place, and characters involved determine whether this is an actual or exaggerated situation. Either way, you may choose to exercise the additional option to fight or flight: communication. When you choose communication, you call on skills of the mind rather than the emotions.

## HIDDEN MESSAGES IN CONFLICTS

Once you decide to deal with conflict through communication, you will need to acquire the necessary skills to understand the other person and to listen to him or her. You will have to communicate your needs clearly. The big step now is to learn to respond without the emotions or, better yet, in spite of them. Many conflicts occur because of an inherent animosity between the two people or a dislike of the situation. Individual differences over the issue have very little to do with it. In communication we not only evaluate our own needs but also try to understand the other person's. Frequently, conflicts contain hidden messages, which are essential for us to discover. All too often we hear only our own inner script and tune out the other person's. We have all heard a scenario that sounds like this.

> # 1: I want to watch the football game.
> # 2: I want to watch the movie.

The conflict here can shift quickly from the basic issue of what they will watch on TV to an emotional reaction by one or both parties. This kind of conflict offers another approach to a simple drama in which one person wants one thing and the other person wants something different. The problem that occurs here, however, is that the needs of each person are distinctly different from the other's. Neither one hears the other's needs. So what happens? They escalate. One person wants to watch the football game, and the other wants to watch the movie, but somewhere along the line the issue gets lost and is replaced by the "you against me" dialogue. Unless they decide to flip a coin, the discussion usually continues something like this:

> # 1: It's an important game, and I'm going to watch it.
> # 2: Oh, what you want is more important that what I want. Is that it?

\# 1: I didn't say that.

\# 2: No, but you thought it. You're selfish!

\# 1: I'm selfish! You're the one who always has to have everything your way.

\# 2: You're a fine one to talk. You never do anything I want.

\# 1: It's always about you, isn't it? You don't care about anybody else but yourself.

\# 2: Me! You're the most self-centered, egoistical. . . .

As you can see, the conflict has escalated. It has nothing to do with TV. It has become a personal attack, each on the other. Now, it's all tied up with *ego* (you think you're more important than I am, ) *lack of respect* (you're selfish), and *past grievances* (it's always about you, isn't it?). These are the hidden messages. From here, it's a short step to name-calling (you're the most self-centered, egotistical. . . ). The original conflict is long gone and of very little importance at this point. How many times have you forgotten what originally started an argument? If you're like most of us, it's happened more than once.

## PERCEPTIONS

A common occurrence in our society today is that simple conflicts over minor issues escalate into full-fledged acts of violence. A recent article in the *Philadelphia Inquirer* (Zucchino 1995) related a scene at a local school. A nine-year-old said to a ten-year old, "Your mama smokes crack. Your granddaddy is dead. And you smell bad." The ten-year-old and another boy retaliated by pointing paper pistols at the nine-year-old's head and saying, "We're gonna blow your brains out." They threatened to "pop a cap"—get a real gun and shoot the boy. Then they punched him. Respect was the issue here.

It is easy to see how name-calling provokes conflict. The conflict itself doesn't cause violence; it's what the conflict represents in terms of ego, respect, and any past experience it may bring up. The inner-city street code, no matter which ethnic group is represented, demands retaliation for slights or perceived slights and equates violence with respect. Rather than work out the problems associated with conflict, young people are all too quick to jump to the "shoot first and talk later" syndrome. When asked the question, "Why resort to violence?" one young teen answered, "peer pressure. Nobody wants to look bad!"

Not all conflicts lead to violence, of course. We see nonviolent arguments occur all around us. The most common one is a simple difference of opinion, which can be about any number of things. There are certain subjects that provoke anger more easily than others. Think about the abortion issue, for example, or assisted suicide. Both of these issues have their passionate supporters on both sides and offer a ready-made conflict. In the theatre the playwright can make use of either of these conflicts for his or her plot. Mary Anne never talks about either of these subjects with her friend Kisha anymore, because she knows how vehemently they disagree. Out of respect for their friendship, they have agreed to disagree and leave it at that.

Two brothers have joined opposing political parties. They discuss politics but only within the boundaries they have set up for themselves. In order to avoid confrontation, they have agreed to discuss the issues only and to communicate in a respectful way. An older adult brought up in another time said she was taught that there were three questions it was disrespectful to ask another person: How much money do you make?, What is your religion?, and Who are you going to vote for in the next election? Politics and religion are still right up there as primary argument instigators. We have all heard intelligent people argue over these topics, with some discussions ending in harsh words.

What about sports fans? You can always get an argument going among them. Sports can provide a volatile topic any time, especially during a World Series, Super Bowl, or Stanley Cup season. It all depends on how seriously the fans take their team allegiance. For example, take two avid rooters for different teams; their conversation can be a good-natured comparison of each team's assets or it can turn into angry retorts to one another. If the objective reality becomes lost and the emotions take over, what happens? A simple difference of opinion can become explosive, as we have frequently seen while attending sporting events or watching them on TV. All it takes is for the conflict to become personal. You've seen it before. How about a baseball game when an umpire makes an unpopular call and the fans discuss it? It might sound like this:

#1: Did you see that stupid call?
#2: Stupid? What's the matter with you, are you blind?
#1: What are you talking about? It was a strike.
#2: What makes you such an expert?

#1: I know what I saw. Any idiot could see it was a strike.

#2: Are you calling me an idiot? You stupid, no-good . . .

Neither one of these fans cares anymore about whether it was a ball or strike. The original issue has gone by the wayside, and the conflict has become personal. The issues now are ego and respect. Both feel that they are not receiving the proper respect from the other. With the emotions running high and the adrenalin flowing, we're back to "fight or flight," and in this case fight usually wins.

## CULTURAL DIFFERENCES

Often cultural differences come into play as well. One ethnic group values a spirited debate no matter how loud the voices become, while in another culture, people show respect for each other by maintaining a soft-spoken demeanor with downcast eyes. Cultural clashes occur frequently when one person misunderstands the other's intent. For example, here in the United States we are taught to look directly at another person, and make eye contact, as a sign of honesty. Yet in some cultures looking at another person directly is a sign of confrontation. The old saying "When in Rome, do as the Romans do" has its basis in respect for another culture. Simple experiences can be real eye-openers in learning respect for cultural differences. Participating in the rituals of another ethnic group or culture can be enjoyable and often enlightening. As one young woman confided after eating a meal with chopsticks with a Chinese friend, "Talk about manual dexterity; you gotta have it or you don't eat!"

Our large cities offer easy access to other cultures with their many festivals, celebrations, and theatre productions. The more we know about those different from ourselves, the better equipped we are to understand them in relation to their world and ours. When we take offense without trying to understand simple cultural or ethnic differences, however, the door opens for conflict and/or violence.

## NATIONAL CONFLICTS

Conflicts among nations are very much the same. Two countries may have a difference of opinion regarding their borders. There is one piece of land, and they both believe it's theirs. This situation is very much like two siblings wanting to use the same car. Usually the older (and stronger) of the two will lay claim as the rightful possessor unless they are able to work out this conflict through compromise or negotiation. Conflict between countries, like conflict between individuals, often involves a challenge to ego or respect or a reawakening of past grievances.

The ego of a country, or sense of patriotism, is perhaps the strongest reason for conflict among nations. How do you feel when someone insults America? The French are notorious for their chauvinism. If you denigrate French wine, you insult the integrity of the country. The English value their heritage as much as some countries value their natural resources. The Russians treasure their museums and cathedrals more than most nations value their wealth. When one nation wants to promote an argument or conflict with another, the easiest way to do it is to attack the country's ego or sense of national or ethnic pride.

For years we've heard about the importance in Asian societies of small talk or polite conversation before any discussion of business issues. What is that but respect? Now look at how countries carry past grievances into political negotiations. How many countries can you think of who are traditional enemies? China and Japan, France and Germany, Israel and Iran. We've all heard something like, "You know you can't trust the _____ . Remember what they did in World War II!"

Past grievances are probably the most obvious of all in promoting conflicts among nations. Germany and France fought against each other in the two world wars. The Israelis and the Arabs have been disputing borders since the inception of the state of Israel. The warring tribes of newly created African nations continue fighting over current boundaries and tribal behaviors rooted in the past. The list goes on of countries with long histories of distrust for one another.

What about families? Shakespeare knew full well the dramatic conflict inherent in family feuds caused by past grievances. Look at the Montagues and Capulets and what their past grievances did to the star-crossed lovers, Romeo and Juliet. Of course this distrust among families is handed down to individuals as well and spills over into our personal lives.

Most of us, unfortunately, are apt to regard someone of another culture, who may be a traditional enemy of our own ethnic background, as a potential enemy. With this built-in animosity stemming from past grievances, confrontation is an easy trap in which to fall. If either one of the other ingredients (threats to ego and respect) happens to appear, the situation is ripe for conflict—no matter what the occurrence or initial problem.

## HISTORICAL DIFFERENCES

History tells us that there are some unavoidable conflicts. Many timeless and universal struggles have been occurring since humans first set foot on Earth. "I am the strongest man in the tribe, and therefore the leader." If another man feels equally strong, his ego is being challenged, and he is also not receiving the proper respect. What does he do? Fight! "This is my land and you have moved onto it." You aren't showing me the respect I deserve because of my ownership. What do I do? Fight!

You insulted my husband, wife, mother, father, whomever. This tells me you have no respect for me or those in my intimate circle. What do I do? Fight!

You tried to steal my woman, man, position in the group, "good name"? What do I do? Fight! In all these cases, the individual not only feels loss of respect, but experiences a blow to the ego as well.

As you can see, conflicts, like death and taxes, don't go away and must be faced. Conflict will be with us as long as humans are around to create it. The theatre is often referred to as "the mirror of society." How much easier it is to deal with conflict as a source of drama rather than as a life-or-death confrontation in the streets.

## THE THIRD RESPONSE:
## COMMUNICATION

Although the most common ways in which we respond to conflict are through confrontation or avoidance, the third response is communication. This third method, which theatre promotes, is collaboration through communication. This collaboration offers choices when dealing with conflict. The solution is no longer either/or. Through theatre we can experience other worlds, behaviors, societies—alternatives to our own way of doing things. In the theatre we practice dealing with conflict as a natural part of life, and learning to deal with it successfully adds a whole new dimension to that life.

"If you can fake it, you can make it!" says one recovering alcoholic. Another responds even more specifically, "If you can play it onstage, you can do it in life." Dealing with conflict onstage makes it easier to do in life. When you play a role, you learn to put yourself in someone else's shoes. In so doing, you often make insightful discoveries about yourself and others.

Conflict is here to stay. What we can do for young people dealing with conflict is to broaden their world and help them understand others as well as themselves. Theatre is a collaborative art that exacts cooperation by its very nature. It teaches a variety of life skills without labeling them as such. When you know only one way to handle a situation, you are locked in, confined. But when you are equipped with several methods of dealing with conflict, you are personally empowered by the knowledge that there are always alternatives in every situation.

## SUMMARY

Conflict is a natural part of life. Without conflict there would be no personal growth or social changes. Conflict is rooted in a challenge to ego or respect, or a rekindling of past grievances. People respond to conflict most often by "fight or flight," but there is a third response: communication. Through theatre we can practice resolving conflicts both inside and outside ourselves. Typical conflicts that occur among young people derive from raunchy rumors, noxious names, fractured friendships, and terroristic threats. It is essential for us to discover the hidden messages in conflicts in order to defuse them. Through the theatre, we can be personally empowered to explore conflict safely and to discover alternatives to violence.

# 2

# Warm-ups to Promote Trust

"If everybody's thinking alike, somebody isn't thinking."
*Unknown*

We like and trust people who are most like us. People feel most comfortable with those who are like themselves, who look like they do, who speak the same language, eat the same food, go to the same church or house of worship, and live in the same neighborhood. The more alike we are, the safer we feel. When trust is lacking, resistance shows up big-time, and anxiety gets in the way of cooperation or learning. Our first task then is to put our participants at ease and create a safe, friendly, nonjudgmental environment in which to work.

This chapter deals specifically with warm-ups that promote trust and cooperation. Each of the warm-ups in this section encourages the participants to share aspects of themselves that might seem threatening in other situations. These activities give people permission to take physical action, to talk, share feelings, and even yell when they feel like it. The warm-ups illustrated break down barriers by developing commonalities among the participants. These activities will help your group members integrate, assimilate, and communicate in order to promote trust.

Trust and cooperation exercises create ways to develop and maintain constructive patterns of behavior. The more we can focus on these and underscore them as a way to solve problems, the less likely it is that violence will be viewed as the only alternative. We practice sports, musical instruments, and speeches, so why not practice ways to resolve conflict without resorting to anger and violence?

## NAME GAMES

If the participants are new to each other, you'll want to start with some name games. An all-time favorite is to state your name and one thing that describes you that starts with the same first letter as your first name. (This is also a good trick for anyone who has trouble remembering names.)

"My name is Pat and I'm pleasant." You can also elicit some simple information with the following: "My name is _____ and one thing I do well is _____ " or "My name is _____ and one thing I wish I could do better is _____ " A line that usually brings out some humor is, "My name is _____ and one thing you'd never guess about me is _____ " or "My name is _____ and one thing my mother always said to me was _____ ."

## SPECTROGRAM

An action spectrogram will get people up and moving. It can also give the director, as well as the players themselves, some specific information. A spectrogram is a line, one end of which represents **like most** and the other end represents **like least.** You can also say one side is positive and the other is negative or even more simply **yes,** I do like that or **no,** I don't like that.

**like most** ——————————————————————— **like least.**

The middle represents undecided or half and half. Players will position themselves along the line according to how they feel about the statement made. For example, ask, "How many people like chocolate ice cream?" Direct your participants to go to one end of the room or the other, whichever area represents their feeling **likes most** or **likes least** about chocolate ice cream.

You can design a spectrogram to elicit whatever information you are looking for. The trick is to intersperse the meaningful questions with others that ask for simple preferences. Ask the questions in quick succession, so that you don't give your players time to think about or edit their responses. In this case let's see how the group feels about conflict in general. Most of the participants will surprise themselves at least once with their response to a question.

### Conflict Spectrogram

1. How many people like pizza?
2. How many people like Chinese food?
3. How many people like liver?
4. How many people like school?
5. How many people avoid conflict at all costs?
6. How many people enjoy a good argument?
7. How many people would like to take a parachute jump?
8. How many people would like to go down in a submarine?
9. How many people always have to win an argument?
10. How many people would like to be president of the United States?
11. How many people think others respect your opinions?
12. How many people can usually work things out in an argument?
13. How many people have to win at any cost?
14. How many people back down when faced with a bully?
15. How many people would rather fight than look bad to others?
16. How many people work well with others ?
17. How many people would rather work alone?
18. How many people think you're an important part of this group?
19. How many people think you're good at resolving conflict?
20. How many people discovered something about yourself in this exercise?

After you have finished with the spectrogram, talk about the experiences people had. What were some of their personal discoveries? Did they surprise themselves at any point? Did they notice if they were usually with the same people? Or were they with different people at different times? Were they ever alone in one area during the exercise? How did that feel? Guide the discussion to get an idea of how the group as a whole regards conflict. Since you have set the tone with physical action to begin, you can move right into another game that calls for the whole group's participation. The following games are fast paced and demand concentration, cooperation, and focus on what's happening here and now. A good game to start is Basket Upset. It's fun! It's simple, physical, and immediate.

## BASKET UPSET

Ask your players to bring their chairs to make a circle, keeping it large enough with plenty of room to move freely across it. There is one less chair than player. The player without a chair is *it* and stands in the center. (The leader can start as the one who is *it* to model the game.) She calls out, "Everyone wearing . . . the color blue . . . change places." (She must be wearing the item she calls out, in this case something blue.) She can name articles of clothing as well, e.g., "Everyone wearing sneakers, change places." (Again she must be wearing sneakers.) She can say, "Everyone wearing a watch (ring, bracelet, nail polish) . . . change places." Players get creative with this and call out articles that are not always observable: contact lenses, fillings in the teeth, underwear, a smile, and so on. The object of the game is for the person who is *it* to get another's chair. Everyone wearing the article called must change places each time. The one left without a chair becomes the next person who is *it* and has to call out, "Everyone wearing _____ change places." The game can get hilarious after a while when a leader is trying to come up with something that hasn't been said and that he has on. Stop the game while it's still fun, and participants will want to play it again and again.

This game requires quick physical action, observation, immediate decisions, and fast moves to another's chair. There's no time to think about any problems or emotional baggage that people came in with. It's a game that's played in the moment and the focus is on the here and now. It sets up a fun-filled atmosphere.

## TWENTY-ONE COUNT

Your players can stay seated for this game. The object of the game is for them to count from one to twenty-one consecutively. This one sounds simple, doesn't it? The trick here is that the players may not speak in any particular order, nor can anyone direct which player goes next. It must be done at random. Each player calls out a number when he or she chooses. If any two players call out the same number at the same time, they start over again from one. Don't be surprised if you don't get past the number four or five the first few times. The game is harder than it looks. What has to happen is that each player becomes aware of the group and the rhythm of the game. This gives the group a chance to try a variety of techniques and different approaches. The game takes concentration and focus. Usually one of your players will want to solve the problem by saying, "Why don't we just go in order around the circle?" Repeat your directive that the players may not go in any specific order or pattern. That's the whole point of the game. Going in order will be their first inclination after the initial frustration of having to start over when two people say the same number at the same time. After a few rounds the group members begin to become aware of each other and listen more carefully. It usually works best when they slow it down, but there are no hard and fast rules. One thing you can count on is a shout of delight when the group succeeds in counting all the way from one to twenty-one without any two players saying the same number simultaneously. This is a game that can be repeated many times. It seems that it's always a challenge and participants are eager to try it again even after they succeed.

## GROUP MOTION

From here the individuals are ready for a more formal challenge to work in a group cooperatively with sound and movement. Divide your participants into groups of eight or ten. Ask them to link arms in a circle and to follow your directions for their group but do it without talking—nonverbally. They must respond as a group and allow the group process to occur.

With their arms linked, ask them to establish a common sound and movement with both feet on the floor. When they have successfully accomplished that task, direct them again with arms linked to establish another sound and movement but this time with one foot off the floor. The third directive is to repeat the exercise but this time moving forward and backward.

You'll want some discussion after this exercise. Ask how the group process worked. Did one person start the motion or did it occur spontaneously within the group? Was everyone comfortable with the sound and motion? Did they feel like doing something else? How did it feel to be a part of the whole and to cooperate with the group?

## GEOMETRIC DESIGNS

Now let's go one step further in the group process. Again divide your participants into groups with an equal number of players. They can be larger this time, twelve to fourteen but no more. This exercise is another nonverbal one, which means no talking once the directive is given. This is an exercise in problem solving but once again it is a group process that is accomplished nonverbally. Ask the groups to begin by forming a circle without talking. Now try a square, no talking. Next, ask for a triangle. This one is the hardest so far, of course. Give players some help if you feel it's necessary. If they were successful with this one, you can give them the "killer." Ask the groups to create a star without talking. Don't try this one if they weren't able to form the triangle.

Again discuss the group process, and give praise where it is due. Of course, leaders will emerge in these group efforts, but for the time being focus on the work of the group and the power of the group process. Talk about how the problem-solving experience occurred or did not. Is it always harder without words, or is it sometimes easier when you don't talk but just rely on communicating in other ways?

## PILOT TO TOWER

More cooperative interaction comes with the next game, promoting trust needed to develop and maintain constructive patterns of behaviors. This is a game that teaches the giving and taking of directions and underscores the value of listening, as well as making sure the two players, the Pilot and the Tower, are on the same wavelength. Each must discover what the words mean to the other. For example, "Take a step," can mean anything from a tiny baby step to a giant leap, so that the Tower learns to be specific with her directions. The Pilot depends on the Tower to give him instructions that he understands and can follow.

Select two players. One stands at either end of the room. One will be the Tower. She is the one who gives the directions and must stay in one place. The other player is the Pilot, who is blindfolded and spun around three times. This disorients him somewhat, so that he must depend totally on the directions he receives from the Tower. Unfortunately, the Pilot has a one-way radio, so he can only receive and not send. In other words, he can receive the directions from the Tower, but he may not ask any questions. That means that the Tower must be very specific and precise with her instructions. Now, as with any flight, there are obstacles in the way of a clear path. You can use desks, book bags, and/or people as your obstacles. It's more fun with people, who can be inventive with their obstacles. They can be trees, bridges, buildings, whatever. Help them to make it difficult but not impossible, and direct them to remain stationary once they have assumed a position. Now if the Pilot touches any of these obstacles during his flight from one end of the room to the other, it's a crash. If the obstacle is a person, that obstacle says, "crash!" Then another Pilot and Tower are selected. If he successfully navigates his path through the obstacles to the Tower, it's a safe landing. This game can be repeated often. Each player will want the opportunity to experience both roles of the Pilot and the Tower. Discuss the game after each round. Which was harder, giving directions or taking them? What was the most helpful about the Tower's directions? Sometimes, you'll hear comments like, "I liked the way she encouraged me the whole time." Or "His voice was very confident and gave me confidence as well."

## THREE X

Everything is experience with young people. The next activity will actively engage them in a three-person problem-solving exercise. This is a simple directive and you want to keep your instructions as brief and open as possible. Have your players count off by threes. Each set of ones, twos, and threes is a trio. Ask them to stand against one wall. Their task is to cross the room from one side to the other but with only four feet touching the ground. Give them a few minutes to figure out how they will complete their task. They may try a few different ways. Then ask each of the trios to cross the room one at a time with only four of their combined six feet touching the ground. You'll usually see the crossed hands of two players making a seat for the third, the wheelbarrow with the two players holding the feet of the third who walks on hands. Or simply one person carries another with the third walking beside them. There will probably be some similarity in the solutions but accept them all as the original thinking that they are.

## BODY TRANSPORT

This activity adds a greater level of difficulty and trust to the exercise above. Divide your players into groups of six or seven. The optimum number in a group is six, but the exercise works with groups of four to seven. The object of this game is to transport each one of the members of the group across the room without that person touching the ground. Each method may not repeat any that has been used before. The groups may use only people not objects. ( For example, they may be tempted to use a chair.) The usual methods include someone being carried by two players crossing their arms to make a seat, or two people holding the hands of the person being carried while two others hold the feet. Another easy one is with three people lifting the person on one side and two others lifting on the opposite side. The interesting thing about this activity is that the players expect to run out of ideas quickly, but they come up with some incredibly creative ways to transport each other. One group lay down on the floor like logs and rolled the person across the room. The log person at the end of the line would come to the front, so that the player who was being carried could roll forward on each log person until she came to the front of the line. This exercise offers not only the physical action of the transport but also stimulates the imagination to new heights of problem solving.

These last two exercises bring the interaction of your participants to a more personal level and provide the interaction that is so lacking in many of their lives. Many young people are in social isolation through computers, TV, video games, and films. These all reduce the chances to know what it means to interact with others, especially touching in a nonviolent or nonsexual way.

## COMMONALITIES

This exercise (Sternberg and Garcia 1989, 30) appears deceptively simple, yet it shows the group members how much they have in common, which in turn promotes trust. It breaks down barriers by developing a common thread. It gives the players permission to talk, discuss, agree, and disagree.

Divide your players into groups of three. It's a good idea to mix them up as well. For example, if you have twenty-one students in the room, ask them to count off by sevens. Then direct all the ones to go to one place in the room, the twos to another, the threes someplace else, and so forth. The point of grouping in this way is that the people who always stand next to each other will have different partners. Once they have all come together in their groups of three, give them the simple directive, "Find any three things you have in common." Further direct them that these commonalities may not be anything obvious or observable. In other words, it can't be that we are all in the gym, because that's obvious, or it couldn't be "We three are wearing sneakers," because that's observable. They must search out their likes, dislikes, similarities, or differences. For example, "We all like Chinese food," or "We all hate liver." These are common likes and dislikes. Ask each of the trios to appoint a spokesperson, and that person will introduce the members of the group and tell us what the three things are that they have in common. After all the groups have stated what they have in common, ask if anyone heard from another group something they also have in common. You'll get a lot more sharing here as well.

There are several of these commonalities that work particularly well in breaking down barriers. Select your trios in a variety of ways to mix your players. You can ask everyone wearing a certain color to get together, or everyone whose birthday is in a certain month or months. Be as creative as you like so that you get a different mix of people. One of the important messages from this exercise is that we all have more in common than we have differences.

For the next round try, "What three strengths do you share?" Illustrate what you mean by offering several of your own perceived strengths. "I have a good sense of humor. I'm intelligent, and I like people." This can provide insight into what individuals consider their strengths and some surprises as well. Again, select a spokesperson who introduces herself and the members of her group and tells us what their three strengths are. Repeat the previous procedure, and ask if anyone else shares the strengths he heard another group mention. You're stimulating analytical thinking here as well as affirming commonalities.

The third commonality is the most revealing of all. Ask, "What three things make you angry?" All three of the participants have to agree on what constitutes a situation that would inflame their anger. This exercise encourages the participants to share things that might seem threatening to them in another situation. It gives them permission to talk about emotions and share some of their feelings. It motivates them to discuss what kinds of things trigger their own anger. Set your ground rules and keep the responses specific to a situation rather than a person. In other words, you don't want, "My old man makes me angry!" because that's a person, but you would accept "Authority figures make me angry!"

Sharing experiences is important. Mutual understanding greatly reduces the potential for conflict. Acknowledge and reinforce the fact that everyone gets angry. It's a natural human emotion. It's not the anger that's the problem; it's how we deal with it that often causes trouble. "I get angry when someone makes fun of me or laughs at me" is a common complaint, as is "I go ballistic when someone lies about me." Perhaps the one that is heard most often in one variation or another deals with respect. "He has no respect for anybody!" or "I get mad when someone starts talking while I'm talking. I want to punch 'em out." Self-disclosure draws people closer together.

This is a good springboard activity to begin role-play scenes that you will find later on in the book. Keep this activity in mind when you reach Chapters 5 and 6. You might want to use this to create some one-liners to ignite the emotions (Chapter 5) or for word plays (Chapter 6). The message here is that you always have choices of how you respond to emotions, especially anger. The more ways you know to respond to an emotion, the richer your life will be and the more control you have in directing your responses.

## SUMMARY

We know and like people who are most like us. Very often we get stuck focusing on external differences rather than taking the time to discover our similarities. Trust comes through knowing other people. Through trust and cooperation activities, exercises, and games we can develop and practice constructive patterns of behavior and ways to accept ourselves and each other without violence as the only alternative. We can begin to build that trust by sharing experiences with others, problem-solving together, and finding the common threads that bind us together as humanity.

# 3

# Theatre Games to Promote Cooperation

Even if you're on the right track, you'll get run over if
you just sit there.

*Will Rogers*

Everyone who has ever participated in any area of theatre knows
the importance of cooperation. In fact cooperation is important in
every facet of life that involves more than one person. Cooperation
takes at least two people who are willing to listen to each other and
move on from there. The more people you have in a group the
more difficult the task becomes. We all know people who are easy
to work with and those who are not. You have probably said to
yourself, "She's great to work with" or "He's not a team player."
What differentiates these two people is their willingness to cooperate with others.

How can we help others learn to cooperate for their own benefit
and for those who work or play with them? Learning is a psycho-
logical experience engaging the entire body. Drama activities and
role play heighten student comprehension of both oral and written
material. Through theatre and theatre games, learning occurs
effortlessly even without our knowing it.

## ACTIVE LISTENING

One major prerequisite for cooperation in any form is affective listening. If you don't hear what the other person is communicating
or don't understand the intent, you are at a loss as to what is

expected of you. Similarly, in the theatre when an actor receives the wrong cue or no cue at all, he's stuck for what to say or do next. Active listening is a basic skill for learning both the art of cooperation and the art of acting. There is another kind of listening that occurs in the theatre also. An actor listens not only to what is said but also to what is left unsaid. This is called *the subtext*. You have no doubt been aware of it yourself at one time or another. For example, imagine that you meet an old friend and he says, "I'm really glad to see you." However, if he's looking past you at who else is in the room and his tone of voice belies his words, you get a different message from the one conveyed by the words. The subtext here is that he couldn't care less about seeing you. Therefore, an active listener listens not only to the text of what is said, but to the subtext as well. This can be called "listening with the whole self."

## COMMUNICATE NEEDS

Equally important as active listening in the art of cooperation is the ability to communicate our needs. Often conflicts occur because one person is unable to tell another what she needs at the time. "I need you here with me" states a simple emotional requirement. Yet some of us find it difficult to state our needs. A girl becomes angry because her friend dashed off to a ball game, but how was he to know she needed him at that particular moment? Too many of us think that the other person should understand our emotional needs just by looking. Unless you're a mind reader you have no way of knowing what other people expect from you unless they tell you. All too many conflicts occur because one person will not or cannot communicate his needs.

Actors learn to make their needs known for the good of the play. "Talk louder if you want my entrance on time. When I can't hear my cue, I don't know when to come in." If that statement had gone unsaid, the actor waiting for the other's entrance would have been hung up on stage alone, a situation that upsets even the most seasoned performer. When needs are communicated clearly, cooperation is much more likely to occur especially when those needs are communicated in a straightforward way without any implied criticism.

Cooperation thrives on the ability to share thoughts and feelings with others without the fear of criticism. Remember there is no right or wrong to feelings. They are what they are, and each of us is the expert on his or her own feelings. One director often says, "I'm angry when you don't know your lines. I don't want to be angry, but I am." She recognizes her feelings as the source of her anger and yet sends a clear message to the actor what effect his behavior is having on her. In addition, she has distinguished between the source of the problem (the unlearned lines) and the owner (the actor).

The theatre experience, by its very nature, promotes cooperation and trust among its members. Each member of the cast is dependent on the other. If one person drops a line, another picks it up. Actors learn to cover for one another whatever the problem may be. They are an ensemble, a team. Every cast knows the truth in the old adage that says "Every chain is as strong as its weakest link." Cooperation is at the heart of all that actors do on the stage. Some members of a cast may even dislike one another, but on stage they are a part of the team that works for the good of the whole. An effective group, like an effective cast, is one in which the group members are communicating with one another, solving problems, and identifying any issues that need airing.

Every successful theatre performance occurs only after days or weeks of practice and rigorous rehearsal, not to mention the hours spent alone by each actor learning lines. Actors exercise both body and mind to keep their instruments in fine tune. By rehearsing in the same rigorous way, students can hone their skills in promoting cooperation through active listening and in communicating their needs in an uncritical environment. Remember that these techniques will be called on during the heat of confrontation, when emotional arousal is high, so they have to be overlearned if they are to be accessible when needed most.

The following games and activities were chosen specifically to generate cooperation among the participants. Some will depend on cooperation between two people and others will involve three or more in a group.

## STAND UP

The object of this exercise is for two people to cooperate physically. Each has to exert equal pressure, one on the other, and rise at the same time.

This exercise for two people is easier if the two people are the same general size, but it can be done with any two people. Direct the players to sit on the floor back to back, with their knees bent in front of them and their arms linked at the elbow. After they are in position, ask them to stand up, keeping arms linked and backs together.

Some pairs will stand up on the first try, while others will fall over to one side or the other and have to start over several times. That happens most often when one person tries to use force to get up or tries to lift the other person. They stand up when they both press their backs against one another equally and push up with their legs at the same time.

Keep the exercise a nonverbal one in the beginning. That way you'll do away with one player telling the other what to do or how to do it or one saying, "It's your fault. You're not doing it right!"

Let your participants change partners and try the activity with different people. Most players can succeed with the exercise with more than one partner, but they will find the task more easily accomplished with some partners than with others. Here is a good opportunity to talk about cooperation and how it is a give-and-take proposition.

## BALANCING ACT

The next exercise illustrates cooperation in the same way as the one above except this one includes the element of trust as well. This one is slower to move into. Whereas in the first activity, similar muscular strength exerted at the same time was called for, in this one it's relaxation that must take place at the same time. The two partners are dependent for their balance on each other. Again this exercise is easier if the players are about the same height but does not depend on that.

Players stand face to face at arm's length from each other's shoulders. When one player reaches across to the other, his fingers should touch the other's shoulders. From that position players hold hands and bring the feet forward so that they are standing toe to toe. Then they attempt to straighten their arms by leaning back while maintaining and/or finding their point of balance. When they find that point, their arms are straight and their bodies lean out and are relaxed. They experience the same balance as on a see-saw. At this point they have succeeded.

However, you may wish to take the exercise a step further. Ask the players to explore their space. If they have their point of balance, they can move up and down and from side to side maintaining that balance with each other. When they succeed with this, you can suggest they close their eyes and further explore their space.

Once again discuss how cooperation was involved in this activity. It necessitates almost the exact opposite kind of body control from the first exercise. Yet, cooperation with a partner is still the key to success. Some people find it extremely difficult to allow themselves to lean back, relax, and depending on the other person to keep his part of the balance.

## BACK TALK

The next game is really a warm-up for the one to follow but can have its own benefits as well. It offers a different kind of physical interaction not using strength or balance but simply communicating by touch.

The players stand back to back. Direct them to carry on a conversation by moving their backs one against the other's. Give suggestions such as, "You can move up and down, sideways, however you wish. Remember, it is a conversation. One person speaks and then the other responds," and so forth.

You'll get some frolicking and laughter on this one, but ask them not to talk until you call time. Then ask each player what she thought the conversation was about. Were their more similarities or differences in their perceptions of the conversation? Ask if anyone can identify what they were feeling during the conversation; were the feelings the same as what they thought the message was?

## CARRY THE BALL

This exercise can add an element of competition if you have several two-person teams playing at one time. Again, cooperation using the body is the goal. If you have warmed up with the *Back Talk*, this will be easy. Players stand back to back in pairs. Place a tennis ball between their backs. The object of this game is for the players to cross the room or any designated area and return without dropping the ball. The longer the area to be crossed, the harder it is to keep the ball between the backs. If the ball is dropped at any point, the players must return to the starting point and begin again.

As you can see, the two players must move in synchronization. If one goes faster than the other, the ball will be dropped because their backs will not stay in the close position to hold the ball there. No doubt there will be a lot of dropped balls and start-overs.

If you decide to use competition in this exercise, designate this as a race. The team who wins should be complimented for their cooperation with one another. Ask the winners what their strategy was and let them talk about it. Discuss what worked and what didn't, focusing on the goal of cooperation. "What did we learn from this?" is always a good question to ask. If someone says, "nothing," remind them that "learning nothing" is a discovery in itself.

## TANGLE

Here's a game that demands problem-solving skills as well as cooperation from the players. Begin with an even number of players, six, eight, ten, and so forth. It works best with eight to twelve people.

Direct your participants to stand in a circle. Reach across the circle with right hands and clasp the hand of a person standing opposite you. Next, reach across the circle with left hands and clasp the hand of a different person. Now the group is in a tangle. The object of the exercise is to untangle the circle without letting go of hands. Yes, it is possible! Everyone in the circle offers suggestions. There is no one leader. Group members come up with as many possibilities as they can. "I think she and I could bend down and let you step over our arms." Sometimes players have to step over or under other people. Sometimes they have to turn around, twist in body contortions, or assume an uncomfortable body position, but they never put themselves in a position where a player is hurt or in pain. The group will try many different patterns and methods for untangling. After a while the players get very creative with their suggestions and all possibilities are tried until the knot is untangled. This can take up to ten or twenty minutes. Some groups give up in frustration, but more often than not, they figure out how to untangle. The beauty of this game is that everyone has to cooperate, and that the group accepts and tries all suggestions that appear possible. Of course, some groups solve the problems more quickly than others depending on their positions that day. That is one of the beauties of the game. It's a new challenge every time even with the same participants, because people stand in different places in the circle or different connections will be made depending on whose hands are held in the circle.

## SQUARE PUZZLES

Some actors prefer nonverbal theatre games to promote problem solving in a cooperative manner, while others argue that the spoken word is always most important in the theatre. That's why directors offer their players a variety of exercises to help them get their creative juices flowing. In the last exercise, *Tangle,* the players explored a variety of possible verbal solutions. This time it's a simple nonverbal game involving group cooperation.

Select several large pictures and have them cut into puzzle pieces. Cut them up into many squares that are all the same size and shape. Unlike jigsaw puzzles, in which the pieces are all different to fit one piece into another, these puzzle pieces are all squares of the same size. The only thing that the players have to go by is the picture they recreate. They have not seen the original picture. Groups of four puzzle solvers work the best, but the exercise can be done with groups of three to five for maximum effect. This is a nonverbal exercise. Direct the players to put their puzzle together without talking. You'll probably hear some grunts and groans, but that's inevitable. This is an excellent stimulant for group problem solving. Again, as in *Tangle,* you'll get a lot of trial-and-error attempts to create the picture. Make sure the picture puzzles you create are all of a similar level of difficulty, so that no one group has an easier time than the others. Most groups accomplish this task, but you can always add a time limit if you choose.

## CHAIR RETURN

Here's one of those trick questions that actors love. It's one of those situations that inspire the comment, "It's so simple when you know how." It offers a simple direct lesson in problem solving.

Direct one player to pick up a chair and hold it straight out from his body at arm's length, so that he is holding it a good distance from the floor. Ask him to put the chair back down on the floor without bending from the waist or his knees or dropping it. (He can't do it, of course.) However, those are the only directions you give him. Allow the actor to try whatever he can to accomplish the task. The simple answer to the problem is for the actor to say, "Help me put this chair down." All he has to do is ask for help from a fellow player. He hands the chair to another, who simply puts it down with no restrictions on bending over. This is a good exercise to point out that sometimes the best and simplest answer to a problem is to ask for help.

## HELP GAME

The help game is a pantomime to improvisation exercise for two people. One actor begins the game by pantomiming a need for help, any need she chooses. It must be an activity or an action in which the first actor must have another person to complete the task or begin the activity. The first person pantomimes her activity. It may be something as simple as trying to pick up a heavy object, which she cannot do alone or trying to hold a door while pulling an object through, or riding a bicycle for two, sitting on a seesaw, and so on. The first person begins her pantomime without words and the second person comes in with a line of dialogue that identifies the problem such as, "Let me help you move that rock."

The first person goes along with the dialogue line even if that wasn't what she was trying to suggest with her pantomime, and continues the conversation. "You're very kind. I think there may be buried treasure under it."

After they have completed the task the first person thanks the second one for his cooperation and leaves. Now it's the second person's turn to begin another pantomime activity in the same way. He will pantomime his need for another person's cooperation. You can continue this as long as your players think of new activities to offer. If you have a time constraint, divide your group into pairs and they can all work at the same time. Ask them to reverse the roles so that both participants get to offer cooperation to the other.

## YARN WEB

This game includes all your players and makes a good closing activity.

The players stand in a circle. The leader has a ball of brightly colored yarn. She holds a string and tosses the ball of yarn to one of the players with the line, "I'm tossing you the ball because I liked your cooperation today by . . . the way you played *Back Talk*," or "by the way you helped us untangle our circle," or whatever. The person who spoke in turn holds on to a piece of the string from the ball and tosses it to another person in the circle with a similar line.

"I liked your cooperation today by the way you played the *Stand Up* game with me." Each person receives the yarn, holds on to an end and throws the ball to another person with a positive comment until everyone has received the yarn. The result is a central yarn web, which illustrates the interaction and/or cooperation of the group, and can be saved or used for display.

## SUMMARY

Active listening is a basic skill for learning the art of cooperation as well as the art of acting. Equally important is the ability to communicate our needs. Cooperation thrives on sharing thoughts and feelings with others without fear of criticism. These theatre games offer practice in cooperation, both verbally and nonverbally, developing trust and respect among the members of the group. Leadership roles are shared, and the exchange of ideas and opinions is respected. Exercises in cooperation offer ways to use the creative imagination, practice problem-solving skills, and develop and maintain constructive patterns of behavior. The very core of theatre and drama is based on collaboration and cooperating with others. These skills are the essence of what the theatre is all about.

# 4

# Unfinished Dialogues
# to Complete

I disapprove of what you say, but I will defend to the
death your right to say it.

*Voltaire*

## STRUCTURE FIRST

In the last two chapters you discovered the importance of warm-ups
to encourage trust in your participants and theatre games to promote cooperation. Once you created that comfortable, nonjudgmental, safe environment, you saw how to encourage group cooperation, trust, and cohesiveness with the proper warm-up activities.
You were introduced to theatre games specifically chosen to
develop cooperation among the players. Up until this point, our
work has been wholly improvisational and spontaneous. Now, we'll
advance a step forward to another level of experience.

This chapter offers a structured beginning with unfinished dialogues to complete. These incomplete scripts will set up situations
between the participants, beginning with simple conflicts and escalating to more dramatic ones. What each person brings to the
scene will determine how it continues and is completed. You will
notice that no description of characters is given, not even gender,
nor is there any location described. The only element the script
contains is dialogue. Each of these scripts includes between eight
and fourteen lines. This design gives the participants a partial structure from which to begin. Remember, the more structure in our
work, the easier it is. Even though you may feel that your group is

ready for improvisations, you will find these dialogues an easy way to ensure that everyone begins on an equal footing with enough structure to achieve success. Some of the participants may continue the dialogues for several minutes, while others may be able to come up with only a line or two. Either way is fine. The dialogue gets them started. It gives the more inhibited group member a chance to participate equally with the extrovert who can't wait to "get up there and do his stuff." The script in hand offers security to the players. They have something to hold on to, both literally and figuratively.

## SIMPLE DIRECTIONS

Begin by asking for volunteers to come up to the front of the room or the designated acting area. Before the players look at the script or begin to read, assign who will read Number One and who will read Number Two. You will notice that there is a simple conflict in each of these beginning dialogues. They get progressively more dramatic and difficult with a deeper conflict as they go along. Call "curtain" as the signal for your participants to begin. Direct them to read the dialogue on the page and when they reach the end of the written script, improvise from that point on. A conflict or problem will be set up, and their own feelings and energy will prompt them to continue. Use your own judgment as to how long you let them continue with their improvised dialogue. Sometimes they will come to a natural conclusion, but at other times you will call, "cut" or "curtain" either because the scene gets too heated or is not going anywhere.

When the scene is over, ask the participants what they thought it was about. Sometimes that will be clear through the spoken dialogue and at other times it will not. Ask them how they felt in the roles they played. What were some of the specific lines that prompted an emotional reaction from either one? What you will get in this discussion is the unspoken subtext of the scene, which will be discussed later on. Ask the audience what they saw in the scene, what they thought it was about. What were the feelings of the audience as they watched the scene? What would they have said in a similar situation? Ask for possible alternative lines.

It's always provocative to reverse roles either before or after the discussion. Make it clear to the two participants that this is a new scene—a new ball game. They can come from an entirely different place this time if they choose. The actor who read character number one now reads the role of number two and vice versa. Again, let it come to a natural conclusion or call "cut" depending on the direction the scene takes. At this point you may want to replay a variation on the scene with characters in mind, i.e., one is the parent and the other the son, or boss and employee, teacher/student, two strangers, two friends, and so on.

## SIMPLE DIALOGUES TO BEGIN

Begin with any two volunteers. It doesn't matter whether they are male or female. In fact the dynamic often changes drastically from two men reading when it becomes two women. When it's a male and female, another additional dramatic element often occurs, producing either conflict or cooperation depending on what the players bring to the script. The same unfinished dialogues can create a dozen different scenes especially when you add characterization to the scenes.

Assign your participants to role Number One and role Number Two, advise them to put the script down when the printed dialogue is finished, and continue from there. Call "curtain" and get started immediately. (You don't want to give them time to start asking questions but want them simply to "go with the flow.")

### Dialogue #1: Time to Go

> #1: It's time to go.
> #2: I don't want to.
> #1: We'll be late.
> #2: I don't care.
> #1: Well, I do care. Let's go.
> #2: Stop bugging me!
> #1: You always do this.
> #2: Me? You're the one who started it.
> #1: _____

Player number one continues the dialogue and continues until it comes to a natural conclusion or bogs down. A natural conclusion could be the following:

#1: Then I'll go without you.
#2: Fine! Go ahead.
(#1 walks out of the room)

Or if the challenge of the line, "You always do this," is picked up, the conclusion might go something like this:

#1: I'm getting sick and tired of you always arguing with me. You never want to do anything I do.
#2: Well, I'm getting sick and tired of you!.
#1: Fine. You don't have to put up with it anymore. I'm leaving.
#2: Good! Go ahead, see if I care.

It can get more heated from here, or number one can leave, whichever. Get the idea?

These unfinished dialogues can go in an assortment of different directions. It will depend on what the participants bring to the scene, whether they add characterization, what they perceive the scene to be about, and any emotional reaction that occurs during the playing.

This technique offers participants not only a structure but also an element of safety, using the script as a distancing technique. ("That's not me—not my problem. I'm just playing a role.") It also offers freedom to react in a way that one might not in real life. In other words, it gives the participants permission to explore some potentially volatile emotions without any fear of consequences. Besides, one thing that everyone discovers sooner or later is that it's great fun to play someone different from yourself.

Go back to *Dialogue Number One* and try it again with different people, and/or different gender breakdown. You and the group decide who the characters are, where they are, and what their relationship is. Once you get started, there's no limit to where you can go with these dialogues. Try the next six in the same way. You will notice that they get more dramatic and deal with more difficult conflicts as they go on. Follow the same procedure as you did with the first dialogue.

### Dialogue #2: Listen

#1: You never listen to me.
#2: You never say anything worth listening to.

#1: That's some attitude.
#2: I don't have an attitude, you do.
#1: Me!
#2: Yes, you. You always try to start an argument.
#1: You're the one who's starting it.
#2: Just shut up, will you?
#1: _____
(Continue the dialogue.)

When the dialogue is over, remember to ask the participants what they thought the scene was about. Don't be surprised if the two participants have totally different ideas about the same scene. Ask what each felt in the role he/she played. Next, ask the audience what they saw, what they thought it was about, and how they felt as they watched. This discussion of what went on and what feelings occurred is very important in understanding conflict. This kind of analysis offers the structure to keep the conflict distanced and will serve as a methodology as we continue into more difficult conflict resolution activities.

Reverse the roles again, Number One reads the role of Number Two and vice versa. Remember this is a new scene. Ask for additional volunteers and play the scene again. It is especially revealing to see how different people deal with the same situation. Discuss the variations between the different players. Did one pair escalate the conflict while another de-escalated it? If so, point out where either change began. What was the precise line that sent the scene in a particular direction? This is an important factor to stress. Identify the line that escalated the conflict. Were there any lines that de-escalated it? Ask for additional alternative lines that might have de-escalated the scene.

Try the following scenes in the same way.

## Dialogue #3: Whispers

#1: What are you talking about
#2: Nothing. Why?
#1: Well, you were talking about something. What is it—a secret?
#2: There's no secret. You're imagining things.
#1: You were talking about something.
#2: What of it? It's nothing that concerns you!
#1: Why won't you tell me _____
(Continue the dialogue.)

## Dialogue #4: Decisions

#1: I don't want to.
#2: Why not?
#1: I just don't want to.
#2: That's no reason.
#1: It's my reason.
#2: That's stupid.
#1: I don't care what you think.
#2: Just wait until you want something from me.
#1: _____
(Continue the dialogue.)

## Dialogue #5: Forget

#1: How could you forget?
#2: I just did, that's all.
#1: But, it was important.
#2: I know it was important. I didn't do it on purpose.
#1: What am I going to do now?
#2: I don't know. I didn't mean to.
#1: You never mean to.
#2: _____
(Continue the dialogue.)

## Dialogue #6: Help

#1: I need help.
#2: You're telling me.
#1: I need your help.
#2: I've given you all I can.
#1: You can't leave me like this when I need you.
#2: Oh, no? Watch me!
#1: You can't do this.
#2: I can't help you any more. You'll have to find another way.
#1: _____
(Continue the dialogue.)

## Dialogue #7: Leaving

#1: Are you leaving now?
#2: Yes, I'm just about ready.

#1: Will you keep in touch?

#2: I'll try, but you know how it is, you get busy and . . .

#1: Yes, I know. It's just that . . . well, we got so close while we were here. You helped me a lot, you know.

#2: You helped me too, but I want to forget about this place.

#1: Do you want to forget about me too?

#2: Not exactly, but. . . .

#1: But, what?

#2: _____

(Continue the dialogue.)

## Dialogue #8: Trust

#1: Why won't you ever trust me?

#2: I don't know. It's just very hard for me to trust anybody.

#1: But, I'm not "anybody." I'm someone who cares about you.

#2: I'd like to believe that.

#1: Why can't you?

#2: I want to, but I . . .

#1: You what?

#2: Do you really want to know?

#1: Yes, tell me.

#2: _____

(Continue the dialogue.)

## Dialogue #9: Important Matter

#1: I need to tell you something.

#2: I'm busy right now.

#1: It's important.

#2: It will have to wait until I get back.

#1: It can't wait.

#2: You don't want me to be late, do you?

#1: This is really important.

#2: All right, what's so important—and it better be good.

#1: _____

(Continue the dialogue.)

## Dialogue #10: Nobody Knows

#1: Come on, let's do it!

#2: I don't want to.

#1: Why not?

#2: I just don't want to, that's all.
#1: You did before.
#2: I know.
#1: It never bothered you before.
#2: I don't want to, all right? Let's forget it!
#1: No, I want to, and if you don't, I'm going to tell everybody you did anyway.
#2: _____

As you can see, in the last three dialogues, the conflict is stronger. However, you will handle these the same way as the others. Discuss what the scene is all about with the participants. Ask about their feelings in the roles. Talk to the audience and ask them what they thought the scene was about and what they felt. Ask for alternative possibilities to the way the scene ended. Encourage the participants to try one of the alternatives offered when they reverse roles or when new players redo the scene.

Why not create some of these unfinished dialogues yourself, or ask your participants to try writing some? Remember to keep the specific conflict vague, so that the players can bring their own experiences to the scene. If you feel confident enough in the work and with the group, try a problem scene. Let your participants discover the problem for themselves and keep it impersonal. You are exploring the many ways of dealing with problems and conflicts, not offering solutions. You're learning to identify lines that escalate a situation. Keep your approach distanced with these unfinished dialogues, and there's no limit to the problems you can explore. The last two unfinished dialogues suggest actual problems faced by some teenagers. These are handled in the same way as the others. Keep the same structure and especially encourage the discussion afterwards with the participants and the audience. No one ever needs to disclose whether any of these situations are his or her personal problem. In this way, various problem situations that young people face can be explored, without using personal experiences or invading anyone's privacy. With these last two dialogues, be especially careful. Maintain the distance. Be sensitive to the possibility that these dialogues may evoke real-life concerns of some participants.

## Dialogue #11: Attitude

#1: You really have an attitude! Why can't you control yourself?
#2: What are you talking about?

#1: You! You always come on like gangbusters You have no self-
    control.
#2: Look who's talking. You're worse than I am.
#1: See, that's exactly what I mean. I try to give you a little
    friendly criticism and you—
#2: "Friendly criticism." You call that friendly criticism?
#1: Yeah, and you can't take it. You always come on with that
    attitude.
#2: I'm really using control now.
#1: What did I say? It's your attitude, that's all.
#2: _____

(Continue the dialogue.)

## Dialogue #12: All You People

#1: All you people are the same.
#2: What's that supposed to mean?
#1: You're all alike.
#2: Like what?
#1: You know what I mean.
#2: No, I don't know what you mean.
#1: Stop playing games. You're like all the rest of them.
#2: The rest of who? What are you talking about?
#1: Forget it!
#2: _____

(Continue the dialogue.)

This dialogue is bound to promote discussion, for we all belong to
several categories of "all you people." Ask your players who they
thought "all you people" referred to. You'll get answers such as
gender, race, age, ethnic background, and so on. We all carry the
emotional baggage of our identity with us, and we all see ourselves
as part of some minority.

"He's talking about me because I'm a woman." "She's talking
about me because she thinks I'm too young to understand." "She
means me because I'm black." "Obviously, she's got a thing against
all men." "He thinks just because I'm white, I'm prejudiced." You
can go on and on with your groups of "all you people." If you read
this dialogue at an AA meeting, who do you think your audience
will identify as "all you people"? If you're at an old-folks' home,
who would it be? How about night school for illiterate adults? Get

the point? Whoever we are, wherever we are, we all belong to several groups of "all you people." We bring our own feelings of inferiority and prejudice to this dialogue and immediately plug into whichever role we play.

This last dialogue demands a thorough discussion afterwards. You can see the possibilities it opens and the discussion it can stimulate. It's best to have your players create characters different from themselves in this one; that offers the added safety of being distanced from the self.

## Dialogue #13: Another Way Out

#1: What's the matter?
#2: I can't take it anymore.
#1: Let me help you.
#2: Nobody can help me. There's only one way out.
#1: What's that?
#2: The end of a rope.
#1: That's no answer.
#2: Well, it's mine. Now leave me alone.
#1: _____
(Continue the dialogue)

You can let this improvisation come to a natural conclusion or you can call "curtain" to conclude it. Begin your discussion with your actors first and ask each one what he or she was feeling in the role. Then open it up to the audience members to share their feelings as they watched the improvisation. Remember to talk about feelings first and then possible alternative lines. After the audience has had a chance to offer input, feelings, and possible alternative lines, reverse the roles and replay the scene. Again, ask for volunteers to play the scene as many times as it seems appropriate and of interest to the group. Don't skimp on your discussion time, especially with these last two scenes. The discussion time is as important, if not more so, as playing the scene itself.

## SUMMARY

These unfinished dialogues offer both a simple structure from which to begin work on scripts and a built-in success factor for participants. They offer participation to everyone involved, the audience as well as the players. All are asked to discuss what they saw, their feelings, and to offer alternative lines for the scene. They gain insight into identifying lines and/or words that escalate a situation and discover possibilities to de-escalate the same scene. Often, two players will have totally different concepts of what a scene was about or what was happening between them. Members of the audience may have yet another concept. How often do our emotions color our perception of what is happening or even what the other person is saying? The connection to make, of course, is that if this misconception occurs in a scene when we have the lines to read, how many times does it happens in real life when we are in conflict or heated discussion with another person?

Most people are not aware of the wide range of their own prejudices, assumptions, or what pushes their "emotional buttons." When we begin to understand this, we also see how conflict can erupt without any apparent reason. Through the discipline of theatre we can practice acting rationally rather than reacting emotionally when our buttons are pushed. The more we understand just what triggers our emotions, the better equipped we are to stay in control of the situation and ourselves at all times.

# 5

# One-liners to Ignite Emotions

When the heart is afire, some sparks will fly out of the mouth.

*Thomas Fuller*

"You *always* do that!"
"You *never* do anything right!"
"How could you be so stupid?"
"It's all your fault!"
"You're no good just like your. . . ." (father, mother, brother, sister, crazy Aunt Lucille)

Sound familiar? Here are some good examples of lines that ignite the emotions. Chances are if you heard any one of these lines directed at you, you would have an emotional reaction. No one likes to be called stupid or compared unfavorably with someone else. That is a real blow to the ego and signals lack of respect. *Always* and *never* are particularly good to start a fight. Those words bring in the whole area of past grievances as well. Once again we see the three challenges come into play to signal conflict: ego, respect, and past grievances.

We all have other lines that we particularly dislike hearing. Ask your participants for lines that disturb them, and suggest that they add those to their personal lists to work out. Try the above lines as one-line beginnings for improvisations and see where they go. (You may want to remind your participants that the improvisation must remain verbal and not physical.) Stop the improvisation when you see the emotions heightened and discuss the feelings of each of the participants.

What we want to do, of course, is to recognize which lines are our own personal igniters. Learn to identify those words as red flags, and say "I won't be caught in this trap." The more we understand our personal response to conflict, the more in control we can be. However, dealing rationally with conflict doesn't come naturally. We all need practice in recognizing what pushes our buttons. We can learn to say, "*You* can't do it to me; only *I* can allow it to happen."

One way to deal rationally with anger when it spearheads a conflict is to separate the people from the problem. This is not always easy especially if you have a relationship with the other person. Is it really Jerry that you're angry with, or is it the fact that Jerry spread raunchy rumors about you? The problem of the rumors is magnified by your friend Jerry's involvement. Where do you begin? What are some alternatives in handling the problem? Generate a variety of possibilities before deciding which action you will take. You want to criticize the behavior, not the person, and let him know how that behavior made you feel. Take a look at the list of *wrong way/right way* lines to explore possible feelings about Jerry. Begin with a line that acknowledges your feelings first, such as, "I thought you were my friend," or, "What I heard really hurt my feelings." Then make your statement.

| **Wrong Way** | **Right Way** |
|---|---|
| I hate you. | I hate what you said about me. |
| You're a liar. | What you said about me was a lie. |
| I'm mad enough to punch you out. | I'm really angry with what you did. |
| I'll get even with you no matter what. | I'm so hurt, I feel like getting even. |

Get the idea? Just like a playwright who must choose words carefully, when you choose your words carefully you're sending the intended message rather than simply a generalized impulse of anger. You are saying what you feel but focusing on the action that triggered your anger rather than the person. Ask your participants to see how many more right way/wrong way sentences they can come up with. In addition, some good positive phrases to keep at the ready are "in my opinion," "the way I feel about it is," and "I see it this way." When you are talking about your feelings and opinions rather than facts, you're the expert. No one else can tell you what you're feeling or what your opinion is. "You're wrong!" sends a message very different from " I disagree with your conclusion." Do some eavesdropping. Listen to the arguments of others and determine how many times the exchange is simply name-calling and general criticizing. See how easy it is to escalate conflict into anger when the words are thrown around at one another helter-skelter. It becomes a vicious cycle when anger distorts our thoughts and our perceptions of the situation. Conflict causes anger, which causes more conflict, which causes more anger until you reach the point of no return.

Blaming others for our anger is a common way to deny our own responsibility. We hold others at fault and refuse to change our behavior. The blame justifies our anger so we won't let go of being angry. What really makes us angry is thinking angrily about things that happen to us. We see the challenge to our ego, respect, or past grievances. We are upset not by the events themselves, but by how we think about those events. And so the cycle continues; we feel the way we think. Some people have what we call a "short fuse," which means they are quick to anger, while others have a "long fuse." It takes them longer to become angry. How about you? Do you have a short fuse or a long fuse? You can take a personal inventory of your anger. Ask yourself, "Where does my anger come from most of the time?"

Of course, we must accept the fact that there are some conflicts we cannot win. AA has a prayer that has proved its worth with many groups and individuals over the years. It says simply and directly.

The Serenity Prayer

God grant me the serenity
To accept the things I cannot change,
Courage to change the things I can,
And wisdom to know the difference.

## ACTION SPECTROGRAM

Let's explore the group's personal response to conflict. Try this conflict action spectrogram (Sternberg and Garcia 1989). (An action spectrogram is a sociometric device that measures choices or preferences.) Remember the spectrogram from Chapter 2. Explain to the group that you will be asking them how they feel about certain things and especially about their response to conflict situations. Imagine there is a line on the floor that goes from one end of the room to the other. One end of the line represents **"like most "**or **"yes"** and the other end represents **"like least"** or **"no."** The area in-between represents the gradations of feelings between the poles. Ask the members of your group to position themselves somewhere on the continuum from most to least as you ask the questions listed below. If they are undecided or in the middle on a particular question, direct them to stand in the middle of the line.

**like most (yes)** ——————————————— **like least (no)**

Remember to ask the questions quickly and suggest that your participants follow their first impulse in answering the questions. Begin with some general questions such as, "How do you feel about pizza, chocolate ice cream, Chinese food, hard rock music, computer games, going to school, working?" Then add your conflict questions to frame this spectrogram to elicit deeper feelings and responses.

1. How do you feel about conflict in general?
2. Do you usually walk away from a conflict?
3. Do you enjoy playing a conflict on the stage?
4. In a conflict would you rather have someone else handle it for you?
5. Would you rather handle it yourself?
6. Do you usually feel good after you have faced a conflict?
7. Do you admire others who aren't afraid to face conflict?
8. When observing a conflict, would you like to intervene?
9. Have you ever intervened in a conflict?
10. Do you prefer your conflict in fantasy?
11. Have you ever regretted not intervening in a conflict?
12. Have you ever intentionally instigated a conflict?

Add some questions of your own, or ask the members of the group to write down suggestions for future spectrograms. Discuss their choices when the exercise is over. Ask participants why they placed themselves where they did. Did anyone surprise himself or herself with a particular choice? Did you find yourself alone with any choice? How did that feel? Did you notice who felt similarly about certain questions? What you hope to help your students discover in this exercise is "What is my personal response to conflict?" The more you know about yourself in regard to conflict, the better able you will be to determine your strengths and to acquire additional skills to deal with conflict not only in the way you want but also in the way you most admire.

## OPPORTUNITY FOR GROWTH

In the theatre we recognize the value of conflict, since all drama is conflict. Conflict is an opportunity for growth except when it bursts into flames of anger. Benjamin Franklin tells us, "Anger is never without a reason but seldom a good one." When anger escalates a conflict, it can transform mere drama into tragedy. We can learn a great deal about emotional control from actors in the theatre. The theatre offers a safety valve in that there is distance between self and role when you act a part in a play. You can act a murderer and feel the anger necessary to play that character, yet still maintain control of your actions. This ability of the actor to participate in a realistic situation and control his or her emotions is a skill that can be learned and applied to real-life conflict. Just as actors rehearse long hours in order to perfect a role, we too can rehearse behavior for dealing with angry conflict situations. The more knowledge we have about anger, ours and others, the more we can be in control of situations. In the following dialogues, direct the players to allow anger to surface and then examine the situation for alternatives to fight or flight. Remember that our third response, which we practice frequently in the theatre, is communication.

Direct the group to count off in pairs and begin their improvisations with the following two lines. A simple conflict is set up, and participants can add their fuel to the fire to heat up the conflict any way they choose.

### Dialogue #1

#1: Give it to me.
#2: You can't have it!.

### Dialogue #2

#1: You did it.
#2: I did not.

## Dialogue #3

#1: I want to leave.
#2: I want to stay.

## Dialogue #4

#1: It's all your fault.
#2: What did I do?

## Dialogue #5

#1: Help me.
#2: I can't.

## Dialogue #6

#1: Would you?
#2: No!

You can play these dialogues over and over again; they will be different with every pair of players. Discuss each one afterward. Offer the players the satisfaction of examining the conflict. What was each of them feeling during the scene? What were some alternatives to their conclusions? What were the factors that escalated or de-escalated the problem? Sharing is vital after a role play of this kind. The sharing allows people to have different opinions, and creates tolerance for one another and respect for differences. People don't get enough experience identifying and communicating their feelings. The more we are able to do that, the better we will be able to understand ourselves and others.

There are times when we have no choice but to deal with a conflict head-on. For those occasions we need to learn offensive as well as defensive strategies. Remember, without conflict there would be no personal growth in individuals or changes in society . Let's take a look at another theatre game that teaches us ways to explore offensive and defensive strategies.

## TAMBOURINE GAME

This game illustrates conflict in its basic state. One person has one goal and the other has another. The group makes a circle, or boundaries are set to keep the action in a limited space. Two players begin the game each with a tambourine in his or her hand. The object of the game is for each of the players to hit the other's tambourine, while protecting his or her own. When one of the players hits the other's tambourine, the game is over. This is an excellent focusing exercise involving problem solving, strategizing, and task orientation. It's interesting to watch the different gender pairs play. The game takes on a different quality with two females (usually more cerebral), a male and female (usually more playful, almost like a ritual dance at times), and two males (usually more athletic and physical). It's as much fun to watch as it is to play, because it's so easy for the observer to see the different strategies put to work.

A few good questions to ask after this game are, "What did you learn about yourself from it?" "What did you learn about your opponent?" "What skills came into play during the game," and "How is this game exactly like life conflicts?"

Controlling your anger while standing up for yourself in a conflict is a skill we all admire. The theatre teaches how to use our emotions for the role we want to play. Let's take a look at how the actor creates his character to meet the intention of the scene. He cannot allow his personal feelings to get in the way of the script. He knows how to use the actor's instrument (mind or emotions, body, and voice). The voice is an easy place to begin. Try the following line using your voice in as many ways as possible: "You're the one." For example, say it as if you mean, "You're my one and only love," or "You're the one who stole my wallet." You can see the difference immediately. See how many different interpretations your group can come up with. How does the intention of the line change with the volume of the voice or the emphasis on each one of the words?

Now try the following conflict scenes in which one person has to stand up to another and ask for what he or she needs, much as in assertiveness training. The object of these scenes, however, is to learn how to harness your emotions to work for you during conflict and to become aware of some of the lines that trigger your anger.

## CONFLICT DIALOGUES

### Mother and Daughter or Son

DAUGHTER: Can I talk to you for a minute?
MOTHER: Now what?

DAUGHTER: I need permission to take Driver's Ed at school.

MOTHER: You're stupid! We don't have a car.

DAUGHTER: But I'd still like to learn.

MOTHER: You're such a klutz, you'd probably run into the first stop sign you see.

DAUGHTER: Not if I learn correctly.

MOTHER: Is one of your boyfriends ( girlfriends) taking it, is that why you want to?

DAUGHTER: No, I just think it's good thing to know.

MOTHER: I get along just fine without driving. Forget it.

## Father and Son or Daughter

SON: Dad, can I go to the lake with some kids over the weekend?

FATHER: What kids?

SON: Some of the guys (girls). Jerry's parents have a house down there.

FATHER: Will they be there?

SON: No, but his (her) older brother will be.

FATHER: I wasn't born yesterday, you know. Sounds like a beer blast in the making.

SON: Jerry's a dependable guy (girl), dad.

FATHER: He's (she's) like the rest of your friends—a bunch of weirdos.

SON: You don't know all my friends.

FATHER: I know Jerry. He's (she's) the jerk with the earring in the nose.

## Boss and Worker

WORKER: Would it be possible for me to have next Saturday off?

BOSS: What for?

WORKER: It's personal business.

BOSS: Monkey business, you mean.

WORKER: Seriously, Mr.( Mrs.) Jones, I need the day off.

BOSS: That's our busiest day. Even a dope like you knows that.

WORKER: That's why I'm asking ahead of time, so that you can get a replacement.

BOSS: You kids are all alike. You only want to work when you feel like it.

WORKER: Could I make up the day another time?

Boss: What's the matter with you? You got a hearing problem or are you just plain stupid?

## Teacher and Student

STUDENT: Could I speak to you for a few minutes?
TEACHER: I'm too busy right now.
STUDENT: But it's important.
TEACHER: Oh, all right. What is it? And make it quick.
STUDENT: I don't understand the math assignment.
TEACHER: Get serious. It's perfectly simple.
STUDENT: Not for me it isn't.
TEACHER: Just stop goofing off all the time.
STUDENT: I'm not goofing off. I just don't understand, that's all.
TEACHER: Don't worry about it.

## Coach and Player

PLAYER: Hey, Coach, will I be starting in the game next week?
COACH: How should I know? It's a week away.
PLAYER: I've been at every practice all season and I feel I deserve more playing time.
COACH: What are you—the coach all of a sudden?
PLAYER: No, but you said you wouldn't start anyone who missed practice, but you did.
COACH: Who are you to tell me how to run my team?
PLAYER: I didn't mean that. I just want to play, that's all.
COACH: I don't need crybabies around here.
PLAYER: What can I do to start on Saturday?
COACH: Stop being a wise guy and get rid of that smart mouth of yours!

After each scene discuss what happened. How was the scene resolved? What are some alternatives to the solution? How many other solutions can you describe? Accept all of the alternatives that are given, no matter how outrageous. The point here is to get in the habit of finding alternatives for every situation. Encourage the group to come up with as many different endings as possible for each situation. Next, ask your players to pick out specific lines that escalated the conflict or de-escalated the conflict for them. Solicit responses from your audience dealing with the same question.

What lines did they hear or what action did they see that caused an escalation in the conflict or de-escalation? Frequently, those on the outside see things that the participants do not. Did either of the participants in the scene appear to become angry? If so, here's a chance to explore it.

Participants can learn to identify those angry feelings and experience them as a signal to slow down. It's easier to slow down early before anger further ignites emotions. Here's where you want to emphasize how we can unlearn old habits and relearn new ones. The secret is to stay in charge. Everyone likes to be in control. You can control your anger to keep the conflict from escalating. Remember the old advice of counting to ten. In other words, call time-out for yourself. Take a few deep breaths and then talk to yourself. You can become your own side coach with lines like "Take it easy," "Don't get upset," "Don't make yourself angry," "Keep those emotions in check."

Ask yourself, "What's really going on here?" What do I want? What does she want? Is there another way of looking at this problem other than my way or her way? Has it become simply a contest of wills that I have to win? Is getting my way more important than solving the problem? Here's where you want to reassess or redefine the problem if possible.

Next ask yourself, "What's one helpful thing I can do about this problem?" Look at it from both sides. What part of this situation can I change? What part of it do I have to work at accepting?

Now direct your players to choose one of the dialogues and rewrite the script. Write specific lines for the character that will escalate the conflict. Also create new lines for the other character that will de-escalate the conflict and underline the key de-escalation line. Ask students to include the inner thoughts or subtext of the character who is in control of his emotions. Label that the *interior monologue.* The rewritten scenes might look something like this:

### Teacher and Student

STUDENT: Could I speak to you for a few minutes?
TEACHER: I'm too busy right now.
STUDENT: Could you give me a time when I could come in and talk to you?
TEACHER: Oh, all right. What is it? And make it quick.
STUDENT: I don't understand the math assignment.

TEACHER: It's perfectly simple.
STUDENT: Not for me it isn't.
TEACHER: How can you be so stupid? (escalation line)
STUDENT: I certainly feel that way sometimes. (de-escalation line)
    (*Interior monologue*)
    (*I will not let him push my buttons. I will stay calm and in control of this discussion. He's probably upset about something else, and I just happen to be here. I'll take a deep breath before I continue.*)
    I guess that's why I need you to explain it to me again.

TEACHER: You're a goof-off. I have more important things to do.
STUDENT: This is really important to me. Is there a time when it would be convenient for you to help me?
TEACHER: Not today. (*Exits*)
STUDENT: (*Interior monologue*)
    (*I will count to ten, and then I'll scream after he's gone. I can't change him, but I can find another solution to my problem that doesn't involve him.*)

Rewrite the other three scripts in the same way and follow the procedure for discussion. See how many alternatives the participants can come up with for each scene. During the discussion, focus on exploring a core of emotional and social competencies such as controlling impulses, managing anger, and finding creative solutions to social predicaments.

## CONFLICT OBSERVATIONS

Earlier you did some eavesdropping to determine what proportion of an overheard argument was simply name-calling and general criticism. Take your eavesdropping a step further and jot down the conflicts you observe this week. Write the date, time, place, and names of the people involved. Pay special attention to arguments you are personally involved in. See if you can identify the words or phrases that ignite your emotions or those of the others. Can you identify the problem in each of the conflicts? Did you remember to separate the people from the problem? Can you identify the *why* or reason behind the situations that bring on conflicts? You might want to ask yourself, "Do I enjoy a good conflict?"

After the group has kept the conflict logs for a week or two, ask them, "What's really going on here? Is there a pattern to your anger or others you observed? Do the same kinds of situations bring us all into conflict?" You might even ask, "Do you enjoy a good conflict?" Have the entire group share their findings. What did they learn about themselves and others? Were they able to identify and label those statements or situations that brought them into conflict?

## SUMMARY

We all have specific lines that ignite our emotions, make us angry, and cause conflicts. Once we learn to recognize these lines or situations, we can control them. When you criticize others, focus on the behaviors and not on the person. The action spectrogram helps us understand how we respond to conflict situations and encourages us to share those feelings with others. When conflict is accompanied by anger, it can escalate to the point of taking over our emotions. The more we know about anger, ours and others, the more in control we can be. What really makes us angry is thinking angrily about the things that happen to us and experiencing a challenge to our ego or respect, or from rekindling of past grievances. The conflict log is a good way to understand our responses to anger and conflict. Everyone needs experience in identifying and communicating their feelings. Practicing impulse control, managing anger, and finding creative solutions to problems we encounter goes a long way to establish self-confidence. Theatre techniques, scripted scenes, and improvisations help us understand that conflict is healthy and can promote personal growth and changes in society.

# 6

# Word Plays, Red Flags, and Stop Signs

> False words are not evil in themselves, but they infect
> the soul with evil.
>
> *Socrates*

Words have power. They can please, hurt, inspire, or devastate us. It's as if words take on a life of their own with a power not found in the letters that make them up. Playwrights know the importance of a single word in portraying emotions or illustrating how a character feels or thinks. This can be particularly difficult for the writer if the word has many different meanings, not to mention connotations. Some words come equipped with a high emotional content. For example, take a word like *change*. The definition that pops into one person's head means the coins in his pocket, while another might think of departing from a usual course of action. The dictionary gives us this definition for change: "to cause to be different." *Change* is a dynamic word because it represents a powerful human action, an action that takes courage to perform.

How many times have you heard someone say, "I wish I could change my . . ." (school, family, friends, girlfriend, job, attitude, self, life)? You've probably said it yourself. This is one of those words that can easily spark improvisation and sometimes serve as a springboard into a full scene.

## WORDS FOR PLAY

In Chapter 4 you saw how the unfinished dialogues could inspire a whole dramatic scene. In those exercises, you had several lines of dialogue around which to structure the improvisations. In word plays you begin with only one word. The first step is to brainstorm the meaning of the word with your actors. You may have to clear up some definitions first. Most words have more than one meaning, especially if you are considering them from several points of view, yours as well as another person's, for example, "What would I like to change about myself?" versus "What would I like to change about you?" Merely looking at the word from a different point of view can change your understanding of the word.

After you've brainstormed meanings of a word, in this case *change,* write each of the sentences below on a separate piece of paper. Fold the papers so the players don't see the lines written on them. That way neither of the two players sees or hears the line until the improvisation begins. Divide your players into pairs, and ask player Number One to select a paper from the pile. She will begin the improvisation by reading aloud the one line, which features the word you have discussed. Player Number Two, the partner, must respond to the line according to his inclination, and the two continue the improvisation until it comes to a natural conclusion or the director calls "curtain" as the signal to stop. Reverse the order and let player Number Two select the next paper with a line written on it. This time, he begins the improvisation with his line of dialogue and player Number One must respond.

Remember to write each one of these lines dealing with change on a separate piece of paper.

### Change

1. Won't you change your mind about it?
2. You'll never change.
3. You'll have to change, that's all.
4. Why can't you change it?
5. What can you change about the situation?
6. You always change your mind.
7. I have to change this.
8. I can't change anything.
9. I change all the time.

10. I don't know what you want me to change.
11. I'd like to change our relationship.
12. There's no way I can change what happened.

Add as many more of these as you like. Once you get the idea, you'll see how easy it is to come up with word plays based on the specific lines you'd like to see explored further. Some other words that work well as springboards for improvisations are the following:

*trap*
*stuck*
*crack*
*sharp*
*fault*
*train* (This one has the greatest number of meanings.)

The word *trap*, of course, can refer to an animal trap, a situation that feels like a trap, or a rattle trap, and so on. See how many other uses you can come up with for the word. Follow the same procedure by discussing the word first and then writing the lines on paper. Remember, if player Number One selects the paper, then player Number Two must respond to it.

### Trap or Trapped

1. You make me feel like a trapped animal.
2. You set me up with that trap.
3. You act like you're trapped in a situation you don't like.
4. That's the oldest trap in the world.
5. Did you set the trap?
6. You set the trap, and I'll get the bait.
7. I might have known you'd fall for that trap.
8. I can't believe you trapped me like that.
9. I like to trap things.
10. I won't let you trap me again.
11. Is it a trap door?
12. There's no way out of this trap.

This exercise once again illustrates how far one word can take us, as well as the fact that certain words have various meanings to different people.

## RED FLAGS

Words can stimulate our imagination, but they can also incite our anger, especially if they are derogatory to any racial or ethnic group. Racial and ethnic problems are a major source of conflict in U.S. schools, particularly in urban areas. By the year 2000, one in every three U.S. residents will be a person of color. Racism and prejudice must be acknowledged. These are the most important variables for students because their daily experiences validate this reality. Prejudice must be acknowledged but not condoned. It is a fact. It exists in the world. How do we deal with it? How do you personally deal with it? How do the students deal with it?

Studies indicate that cooperative activities, working together in a noncompetitive environment, is one of the most effective ways to help students attain more positive racial attitudes. Here's where the theatre can teach the rest of the world a valuable lesson. Once again the teamwork necessary to present a play takes the cooperation of everyone involved. Anyone who has ever directed a play with a diverse cast knows how quickly racial and ethnic barriers melt away through the spirit of cooperation rather than competition.

In the last chapter we examined *One-liners to Ignite the Emotions,* but sometimes all it takes is a single word or label. These are trigger words or labels that arouse our emotions. Let's take a look at the words below and create a spectrogram based on our feelings and/or reactions to the words. You will remember that a spectrogram examines choices or preferences with one end of the line representing **like most,** or in this case **easily accept,** and the other end of the line represents **like least.** In this exercise it will represent **reject totally.** Once again the center will represent **undecided** or **no preference**

**easily accept** ——————————————————— **totally reject**

This spectrogram will measure your feelings toward the trigger words and/or labels below. Begin by asking the question, "Which words do *you* freely *use* to label others?"

1. nigger
2. spick
3. nut
4. kike
5. retard
6. junkie
7. wuz
8. nerd
9. bitch
10. ho
11. honky
12. stupid
13. wop
14. garbage head

Now repeat the spectrogram once again using the words above, but this time ask your players, "How do you feel when the following words are used about *you* or in reference to *you?*"

Discuss how the second spectrogram was different from the first. What were the students' feelings in both of them? Discuss feelings that any of these words aroused in the participants. Did anyone feel that flame of anger occur in response to one of the words? Which words were your personal red-flag signals of danger?

This discussion can provide the opportunity to consider ethnic diversity as a positive element in society. Point out how it enriches our nation and increases the ways in which we can perceive and solve personal and public problems. Are there some ways we as individuals can participate in a variety of ethnic cultures? Do ethnic conflicts sometimes occur because we misunderstand the meanings behind certain words? Ask for examples.

However, let's not confuse anger with conflict. Conflict can bring about positive results. It is an intrinsic part of the human condition, especially in a pluralistic society such as ours. Conflict is often a catalyst for social change as well. It's important to note that conflict between ideals and realities always exists in human societies. Focus on any conflicts your participants felt during the spectrogram you just did. Perhaps the conflict a player felt could be the impetus to change or at least examine one of his or her own prejudices. On the other hand, some conflicts can lead to anger. And when anger blasts forth with no stops, we are no longer in control of our emotions or ourselves. How do actors portray anger in the character but maintain control in the self? One of the ways is by rehearsing a reaction contrary to the one he or she feels, a technique all our participants can learn from.

## DETOURS

Once we become aware of what conditions cause our red flags to unfurl, we need to discover some personal *stop signs* to use for ourselves. The first step is to analyze our own anger, to understand what makes us angry. The exercise below will help your group make their own discoveries about anger. Ask your players to put their words into action. Direct your participants to form two lines facing each other. Each person repeats the line and adds his answer to it as he crosses over to the other side. This gives your people a chance to physicalize their answer, to walk as they talk. You may want to model the first two or three sentences yourself to show your participants how the action helps the words flow, and be honest about what makes you angry. It's equally as important for you, the director, to share your feelings as it is for the players to share theirs. All the players will cross from one side to the other during the course of the exercise.

1. I get angry when . . . (The player crosses over to the other side as she finishes the statement.)
2. When I'm angry, I usually . . . (cross over/answer)
3. People make me angry when they. . .
4. Parents make me angry when they . . .
5. Teachers make me angry when they . . .
6. One thing that really makes me angry is . . .
7. When I get angry, I feel like . . .
8. The last time I was angry I . . .
9. I control my anger by . . .
10. I deal with another person's anger by . . .

Talk about what the students discovered about themselves and others. Keep the discussion judgment free. Did anyone have difficulty in finding something that caused anger? How did people feel about their own anger and that of others? Of course, the most important question is "I control my anger by . . . You probably had some answers such as, "I don't control it," or "I punch 'em out." Here is an area where the theatre offers techniques to cope with that anger. No one likes to be out of control or to be around others who are out of control. The participants can learn to play the role differently. The first step is to use *stop signs* to deal with anger before it reaches the point of losing control.

## STOP SIGNS

Let's take a look at the anatomy of anger. The more you know about it, the more you are able to control the situation. As previously mentioned, blaming others is one of the prime elements of anger, allowing us to rationalize. If we can blame others, we don't have to change our own behavior. Instead, we can hold on to our anger. What really makes us angry though is thinking about it. That adds fuel to our fire. Our thinking about a situation escalates our anger more than the situation itself. This comes from our need to control.

"I want my own way!"
"I must have my way!"
"I'm entitled to get my own way!"

Each one of those feelings escalates until it's too late. It's easier to slow down before your anger gains so much momentum that you can't put on the brakes. Listen to those angry feelings. Let them be your signal to pull out your *stop signs* to help you slow down.

Take a look at the role play scenes below that illustrate the way anger grows. Player Number One is intent on blaming player Number Two and is determined to get her way, while her anger escalates. Play it out and see where player Number Two goes in dealing with the need of Number One to control the situation.

#1: It's your fault!
#2: It is not.
#1: Oh, yes, it is! You started the whole thing.
#2: Don't blame me.
#1: You're the only one to blame.
#2: What about you?
#1: Oh, no you don't. It's your fault. Admit it!
#2: _____

What options does player Number Two have? A problem generally offers three options: solve it, live with it, or get away from it. If Number Two allows the other player's anger to infuse him, he very well could feel pushed against the wall and have to lash out in a violent manner. Unless he can find a way to defuse his own anger in order to defuse the other person's, Number Two is probably headed for a fall.

Play the scene out several times and see what options different actors can come up with. Be sure to discuss feelings of the participants after each scene. Notice some of the variables in each of the scenes. Did your players try to find out exactly what the problem was? Were feelings heightened by what the person thought was the problem? Was there any evidence called for or presented by either side? Were questions asked such as "Who said so," "Is there another way to look at this situation," "Where is the evidence," "Why are you so angry about it?" If someone was able to defuse the anger, what were the techniques he or she used? How do tone of voice and facial expression affect the anger level? Did body language add or subtract from the conflict?

Try the scene again and add one of Number Two's new responses. Each one of these lines offers a way to defuse Number One's anger and begin to resolve the conflict. Each of the six lines below illustrates one of the stop signs we can use to control our own anger.

#1: It's all your fault!
#2: It is not.
#1: Oh, yes, it is! You started the whole thing.
#2: Don't blame me.
#1: You're the only one to blame.
#2: What about you?
#1: Oh, no you don't. It's your fault. Admit it!
#2: _____
#2: Okay, I admit it. Are you happy now?

********************

#2: Look, I know how you feel, and I'm really sorry.

********************

#2: I wish I could change what happened, but I can't. What do you suggest?

\*\*\*\*\*\*\*\*\*\*\*\*\*\*\*\*\*\*\*\*\*

#2: Why don't we both count to ten and start over again.

\*\*\*\*\*\*\*\*\*\*\*\*\*\*\*\*\*\*\*\*\*

#2: I'm afraid I don't know what you're talking about.

\*\*\*\*\*\*\*\*\*\*\*\*\*\*\*\*\*\*\*\*\*

#2: I'm going to slow down before I get hot.

Of course there is no one way that will always defuse anger, yours or somebody else's. There are no easy answers, but the more we try or rehearse a variety of approaches and solutions, the more apt we are to have them at the ready when we need them.

Let's take a look at the stop signs we used to try to defuse anger.

1. Accept the situation as one you can't change. ("Okay, I admit it. Are you happy now?")
2. Try to empathize with the other person. ("Look, I know how you feel, and I'm really sorry.")
3. Accept the responsibility and ask the other person for suggestions. ("I wish I could change what happened, but I can't. What do you suggest?")
4. (oldie but goodie) Take a deep breath and count to 10. ("Why don't we both count to ten and start over.")
5. Dispute the thinking. Where is the evidence? ("I don't know what you're talking about.")

## IN ROLE

Just as an actor learns to shift gears or change direction in his acting, so can our players learn to use these acting techniques to defuse anger and cool down. Don't underestimate taking a deep breath. Actors depend a great deal on their breathing for characterization. They know that they can create a look of agitation by breathing faster, as well as calm down with slower, deeper breaths. A simple first step in defusing anger is to take several deep breaths. You can combine that with counting to ten.

"Centering" is an acting term that means focusing the breathing, the body, the mind, and the emotions all on one point. It is a kind of pulling together of all the elements of the actor's instrument to focus on the here and now.

The Quakers use a technique they call "tuning out." A Quaker friend explained it this way: "I simply shut down and center myself. I send my thoughts and energy someplace else away from the scene of what is happening."

Remember to ask yourself, "What can I do about this situation? What are my alternatives?"

The message here is loud and clear. We can borrow many of the actor's techniques to control anger and learn ways to defuse that of others. One student named Ray says he likes to use humor when dealing with anger. In fact, he had to laugh at himself when he told us about the line he came out with last week. There was a tussle in the hall and he hollered, "Excuse me, but did someone get in the way of your elbow?" The antagonist looked at him and laughed. Humor doesn't always work, but it's worth a try.

## SUMMARY

Words are powerful and have the power to help or hurt us. They have a variety of definitions and connotations as well. Certain words make good springboards for word plays that are fun to improvise and also offer insight into how we comprehend them. Conflict should not be confused with anger, for conflict can bring about positive results. The old adage "Sticks and stones will break my bones, but names will never hurt me" is only partially true. Too often labels or names with racial or ethnic slurs show disrespect and incite anger. Prejudice must be acknowledged but not condoned. We need to identify our own warning signals or red flags, so that we can practice our personal stop signs that help us deal with anger before it flies out of control. The more we know about our own anger, the more we are able to control it. We can learn a lot about control from actors in the theatre. We can rehearse a healthy response to anger situations, and we can learn to play the role of a calm person even when we aren't feeling that way inside.

# 7

# Problem Cards for Improvisation

There is nothing either good or bad, but thinking makes it so.

*Shakespeare*

Playwrights tell us that there are only six basic plots and everything else is a variation thereof. The same can be said of basic human problems, especially those of young people. The cast of characters may change but the plots or problem conflicts are much the same, repeated again and again. A drama therapist friend who has been working with adolescents at risk and adults for the past twelve years states, "People change; problems don't."

Take a look at the problem cards below; they were written over the course of a year at several different schools and facilities by young people participating in drama sessions. Notice how often certain themes repeat themselves. Similar conflicts appear in different words. Each of these cards was written anonymously on a three-by-five file card in response to the directive, "Write down a problem you would like to see us work on in our session today. Don't put your name on it. It will be anonymous, and no one else will know who wrote it unless you tell us." This anonymity offered a large measure of safety for the participants. This technique allowed the players the opportunity to divulge problems for exploration that they might not bring up otherwise for fear of punishment or retaliation by their peers.

Begin by reading aloud all of the problem cards below. What are some of the most common themes and recurring problems? As you will notice, one of the most basic issues deals with communication: with family members, friends, enemies, or those in authority. Along those same lines comes the difficulty of saying "no" and/or standing up for oneself. Another prevalent problem is anger or fighting and how to control the inclination. Closely associated with that is impulse control. Several of the cards deal with feelings of guilt, others with trust, and a few with attitude and even depression and suicide. Another oft-repeated theme is lack of self-esteem. Several cards deal with pregnancy. Discuss these issues and any others that may come up during the reading of the cards.

You will find over one hundred problems listed below. The problems below were written anonymously by young people between the ages of ten to eighteen from several different schools including residential facilities. They were edited only for spelling and clarity. Otherwise, all of the cards were copied as they were written by participants in a drama group.

## PROBLEM CARDS
### Group # 1

1. Dealing with my temper.
2. When parents always take sibling's side without even knowing the problem.
3. Attitude.
4. Depression.
5. Get along with brother, sister, mother.
6. To try to tell your mother that you don't want her to get married.
7. How to talk to your mother and father.
8. My best friend is pregnant. What should I do?
9. My friend wants to borrow my new dress, but the last time she borrowed one she ruined it.
10. Fear of turning eighteen and being on my own.

### Group # 2

1. My problem is trying to be everyone's friend at the same time.
2. Fights with parents over style.
3. My mom got mad at me and ever since hasn't trusted me.
4. I love somebody and I can't show them.

5. How to ask my friend if she stole my boyfriend.
6. How to say no to people.
7. My friend is jealous of me. I go out with her boyfriend, and she thinks she's better than me.
8. I have a problem with saying no to men. Every time they ask me to have sex I just do.
9. My ex-boyfriend is pissing me off and trying to make me jealous.
10. I love guys too much.
11. My friends call me a perpetrator. How can I deal with it when it makes me mad?
12. I have one friend that is supposed to be my friend, but she is a liar, perpetrator, and traitor. She also starts trouble. How can I stay away from her? How?
13. My friend is jealous of me.
14. I'm depressed because my grandfather died yesterday. How can I deal with it?
15. My problem is drug abuse.

## Group # 3

1. Being helpless (same card):
   1. suicide
   2. pregnancy
   3. drugs and alcohol
   4. running away from home
   5. when you think someone is mad at you
   6. child abuse
2. My friends turned against me for no reason. They tell other people not to talk to me. That gets me upset then I want to kill myself.
3. Confusion.
4. I'm going to be an adult soon, and I'm not sure what I want or how to handle it.
5. When I'm serious to someone and they laugh about it or smile.
6. People say I do things when I don't. How can I deal with it?
7. Someone wants to know something, and I'm afraid to tell them because it's embarrassing.
8. Being able to express feelings.
9. My mom gets mad at me and starts to bring up the past.

10. It's a problem with my sister's friends.
11. Me and my mother had gotten into an argument because she's getting married again.
12. Nosy. I am a very nosy person and I get into everybody's business.
13. When people act too tough and they think they can own the whole world.
14. Never to be suicidal again.
15. What should I do about a snobby sister?
16. Problems—1) suicide, 2) running away, 3) freedom
17. What would you do if someone tells you to do something, and you don't know how to say no?

## Group # 4

1. I'm a traitor to my friend, what should I do? (and she finds out?)
2. Problems—1) pregnancy, 2) child abuse, 3) drugs and alcohol.
3. Saying no to somebody when they ask me to do a favor that I don't want to do?
4. Children thinking of suicide.
5. Problems with impulses and not being able to hold back.
6. Children being disrespectful and mouthy to adults.
7. You suspect your brother of using drugs, what do you do about it?
8. You're asked by a friend to run away, and you know it's wrong. How do you tell them no without being a nerd?
9. If you love someone, how do you tell them?
10. Sometimes I really don't want to study even when I know I should.
11. I've given my mother a lot of grief, and now she is distrusting of me.
12. What do you do when someone has violated your rights?
13. What do you do when someone lied to you?
14. A person pretends to be your friend, but then your so-called friend is talking behind your back.
15. DEPRESSION (caps are the writer's).
16. My friend told me she is pregnant and she wants me to tell her what to do. I think she should tell her boyfriend and tell her parents, but she won't.

## Group # 5

1. Someone takes up a nasty attitude with you when you have done nothing wrong.
2. Problem—fighting.
3. Someone is provoking you into a fight.
4. People bugging me and hitting me. They keep it up, and I cannot let them do that anymore. I'll hit back.
5. Whenever you have a problem or want to talk, no one talks to you. They never have time.
6. Someone has a bad attitude at you.
7. What can you do if people tell you to do something and you don't want to do it?
8. Cursing a lot.
9. When you lose someone that you love.

## Group # 6

1. Your boyfriend isn't liked by your friends, should you drop him?
2. I have an attitude problem. Everything is boring.
3. I want to see better relationships between people.
4. Somebody is always butting into your business.
5. Drinking problems.
6. People minding my business who think they are better than another person.
7. Fighting.
8. Flashbacks.
9. I'm not allowed to smoke but I want my cigarettes now.
10. Girls being impatient and not waiting for things.
11. Death.
12. My problem is boys and love.
13. I'm all alone and no one seems to care. All the kids tease me, and my parents say it's all right. What should I do?
14. I can't seem to trust anyone when I'm in a relationship.
15. Self-abuse.
16. Conflicts at home.
17. I have a problem saying no to men and boys.
18. I have a problem with getting along with my mom.

19. You don't tell a friend the complete truth about a potential problem, because you don't want to get in trouble. You would rather get in trouble later. Now you feel guilty about not telling.
20. I have a problem, one of my sisters is a snob.
21. Your best friend leaves and you don't know how to handle it all.
22. Your friends are planning to run away and you really want to go but something is holding you back.

## Group # 7

1. I have a friend who got pregnant and it is pissing me off.
2. What if you really try to help someone by writing a letter to their parents and you thought it was the right thing to do? But afterwards she stops talking to you and doesn't like you anymore.
3. How do you react when a someone is banging and yelling in her room and making a lot of noise?
4. How can you handle a situation when someone tries to put you down—calls you names "stupid" and "retard" and they make fun of you?
5. I've tried to smother out my mom, but yet I still want to be around her.
6. When you make an effort to do something and find that it was done and all your effort was for nothing.
7. I have a problem when my friend does something wrong to me and she knows I am going to find out, but she tries to deny it.
8. You're pregnant, but you're afraid to ask for help.
9. Want to feel more accepted.
10. Need more love and romance. Feel suicidal!
11. I can't think right.
12. My friend comes to visit me from the hospital, but my parents reject him as not the right kind of friend for me.
13. You go home and have your old boyfriend over and your new boyfriend from your new school comes to visit.
14. I need to work on my problem of always thinking someone is mad at me.
15. Self-esteem.

16. People pushing a certain religion on you when it's not the one you believe in.
17. How can I get my girlfriend to stop arguing and fighting?
18. I feel left out!

## Group # 8

1. I'm tired of people fighting and pissing me off and people stealing my stuff. And I'm a little suicidal and depressed.
2. I can't get my self-esteem up.
3. Want some people around here to knock off the attitude.
4. How to stop having temper tantrums of something I can't do anything about happening.
5. What do you do when you go home and your family does not pay attention to you and you feel worthless?
6. I want to learn to be more relaxed.
7. You want to ask a guy out but you're afraid he'll say no so you turn to your best friend.
8. I'd like us to have a greater willingness to discuss real problems—not necessarily the biggest ones—but real ones.
9. Teenage pregnancy.
10. I would like to see the people in this place develop better relationships.
11. What do you do when you are out with friends and they want to go somewhere that something bad happened to you and you don't want to go but you don't want to tell them what happened?
12. Your mother walked out on you, then says she loves you.
13. Prejudice.

Let's take a look at some of the problems that appear frequently on this list. For example, one of the problems that occurs repeatedly is pregnancy. Set up an improvisation with four people. One character can be the girl who is pregnant. Another could be a friend who counsels her to get an abortion. Another friend could be against it. The fourth character could be the boyfriend, the mother, or a counselor, depending on how the improvisation will be played. The conflict here is that the pregnant girl is undecided as to what to do about her pregnancy. Her friends verbalize the two sides of her dilemma to compound her problem. If the group decides to use the boyfriend in the improvisation, he can decide what stand he wants to take. He may agree with one or the other of the girl's friends or he may take a different tack all together, e.g., "I don't believe you. I don't believe I'm the father. I'm outa here," or "I love you and want to get married." How he views the problem will be his choice. Whatever choice he makes will further add to the girl's conflict. When the improvisation has clearly defined the problem, ask the audience to offer additional possible solutions. Ask the players to select the one they want to use and play out that scene. The audience may want to bring in another actor to portray a parent or other adult to help with a possible solution. The important part of this process is discussing the possible alternatives available to solve this problem. (Note that not all problems can be resolved. Sometimes the solution lies in the discussion of the issue and the acceptance of the problem. Very often the realization that others share or have the same problem can alleviate the inner personal conflict.)

Another problem that appears frequently on the list is being able to say no when you don't want to do something. Ask your players for an example situation. One problem that often surfaces here is dealing with an invitation to a party with friends. However, the person knows there will be drugs there. Add the complication of a promise to parents about no parties with drugs. Select four players. One can take the role of the person who wants to say no. The second player can be the host of the party who invites the group, and the other two can be friends going to the party. Player Number Two extends the invitation, Three and Four accept and turn to player Number One for his answer. There's the problem. Now what?

Ask for suggestions for how this conflict can be solved. Some answers might include, "Just say you're busy." "Say: I'm sorry but I can't. You don't have to give a reason." "Go anyway but don't use." "Just go and enjoy it!" And you're bound to hear, "Just say no." Player Number One makes her selection and they replay the scene.

Your players are in groups of four or five. Give them a blank three-by-five card to write out the problem they will improvise. Give your players a few minutes to cast the roles and make their general plans for the improvisations. (Remember, improvisations are not rehearsed beforehand. Actors are assigned roles and general plans are made for the action of the scene.) When everyone is ready, each cast will set up the improvisation and play it out for the rest of the group. After each improvisation, ask the other players to determine what the problem was. When the correct problem is guessed, one of the cast will hold up the card and read it aloud. Once the problem is correctly identified, discuss possible solutions. Let the group who improvised the problem select the solution they feel is the best and act out that one. After they have played out their solution, ask your actors to comment on how that solution felt to them.

These lines offer enough problems to keep you busy for several months, playing out as many as your group can handle. However, our next step is even more important in the overall scheme of conflict resolution. When you're ready, ask your group to write out their own problem cards. They'll get a good idea of the kinds of problems that other young people have from the ones they've already worked on. Hand out blank three-by-five-inch cards and a pencil to each of your players. Explain that the cards will be anonymous. No names are to appear any place on them. Give them a few minutes to collect their thoughts and write down the problems they would like to see worked on. Tell them that the problem doesn't have to be one of theirs. It can be a problem that they have observed or that a friend is going through (another safety net for the individual). When everyone is finished, collect all the cards. Drop them in a hat or shuffle them as you go, so that your group is assured of their anonymity. Tell your players that you will review the cards for common themes as an easy way to begin. Usually you can find several common themes among them. That also gives you the opportunity to remove any cards that may be inappropriate for improvisations. Pull out all the cards that deal with the most common themes. Offer your players several choices for the themes they'd like to work on during this session. Go with the group's choice of the theme for today and pull out all the cards that deal with that particular theme

Follow the same procedure with these improvisations as you did with the problems listed previously. Divide your players into groups of four or five. Ask them to select one of the cards, face down, of course, for their improvisation. Give the players a few moments to plan their improvisations and then present them. Again, after the improvisation sets up the problem, the audience identifies the problem and guesses what the card says. This can very often become hilarious when the audience tries to guess the exact words. Ask your actors to agree to accept the answer if it's close enough.

When they have successfully targeted the problem, ask your audience for possible solutions. The actors pick out the one they want and improvise it. Then ask them, "How did the solution feel to you as you acted it out?".

This activity is worth repeating as many times as you like. It offers a safe way of dealing with existing problems without the fear of being identified as the person who has or wrote the problem. The preceding list enumerated a variety of young people's concerns so it should be easy for your participants to offer some of their own issues. Acting out a situation is so much more meaningful than talking about it.

"I really get into it when I'm playing a role. It's like I have the same feelings as when it really happens," a young woman named Diane stated. This is a comment heard frequently in this kind of work.

Another favorite response came from a student named Dave, "I never thought I could speak up for myself like that."

Other comments frequently heard are, "Now I know how my mother feels," or "Now I understand why he's mad at me,"or just plain, "I never thought of that." When you hear comments like these from young people, you not only see the power of drama but also feel it in action. You literally step into another person's shoes.

Don't forget to keep in mind some of the more dramatic or interesting plots and characters that evolved in your improvisations. You may want to explore them further when you reach Chapter 12, which discusses how to write your own play.

## SUMMARY

Problem cards are a safe way to bring forth actual problems of your group within the safety of anonymity. Review the cards offered in this chapter as examples before you begin to create your own. Once the problem is defined, ask for suggestions for the solution. Select an appropriate alternative and act it out. After the replay, ask your actors how they felt about the solution they played. This gives your actors the opportunity to generate new conclusions for their dramas and also gives them practice in creating different solutions for life situations. In addition, most players gain insight into their own problems through this work, even if it's only to realize that their problems are not unique—a lot of other young people share similar questions, doubts, and dilemmas.

# 8

# Group Problem-Solving
# Scenes

Many of us are more capable than some of us . . . but
none of us is as capable as all of us.

*Ziggy*

Working together in a cooperative setting is what theatre is all about.
Theatre plunges us into dramatic life experiences that run the
gamut of human emotions. It teaches us ways to solve problems
and/or behave in a crisis situation without the fear of consequences.
Theatre experience offers us "practice for living" (Way 1967). Often
it serves as an excellent model for the rest of society. Indeed Maxwell
Anderson, the famous playwright, said, "The purpose of the theatre
is to find and hold up to our regard what is admirable in the human
race." Not all plays or playwrights follow that precept in our theatre
today, but it's nice to know that some do.

Once problem-solving skills are in place, conflict resolution
becomes an exercise in using those skills. More and more schools
are introducing some form of problem-solving skills instruction
into their curricula or extracurricular activities. One program in
Cheltenham, Pennsylvania, has a demonstrable track record. In
June 1997, more than five hundred teams from nearly sixty school
districts in the state of Pennsylvania competed in the 1997 Future
Problem-Solving International Conference in Ann Arbor, Michigan. Also participating were teams from all over the United States,
Canada, New Zealand, and Australia. The competitions were in two
categories, one for middle school and one for high school. Two of
Cheltenham's teams, one from the middle school and one from

the high school, went on to place in the top fifteen at the international competition (Barnhardt 1997, Mc1).

How does Cheltenham's program work? Students are given a general topic to research. They gather facts and pore over studies and texts, not knowing exactly how they might have to use this information. Then, at a competition, they are handed a scenario and locked in a room for two hours. In that time, they must analyze problems in twenty different categories and choose the one that best addresses the underlying issue in the scenario. Every team has four members, each of whom adds his or her own strength. Typically there will be a creative nonconformist, a quick thinker, an organizer, and one member who balances the rest. They brainstorm solutions, develop criteria for evaluating their ideas, and ultimately solve their problem. Their conclusions are written in essays and performed in three-minute skits. Here is the group's opportunity to dramatize their solution to make it more meaningful to themselves and to those watching. The youngsters are scored at every step.

Problem solving has been a part of regular extracurricular activities in the Cheltenham district for almost twenty years. The high school coach Scott Eisner said, "Everyone who's been involved with it can see the benefits. It teaches students how to think, how to research . . . how to take a wide range of information and choose what's important and relevant to the problem at hand." Once problem-solving skills are in place, conflict resolution comes more easily.

By now your players are familiar with improvisation and dealing with role-play scenes that explore problems and emotional reactions. The next step is to move ahead with group problem solving within the structure of a scene. Each actor will have the opportunity to coordinate the scene, to be the problem solver (very much like the Cheltenham team player who "balances the rest"). In the theatre we call that person the director. Every good director listens to the actors and knows that often she gets good advice or suggestions from the actors as well as relying on her own insight. Communication among the players and the director is vital for a successful performance. Frequently, racial and ethnic barriers are completely forgotten. This kind of experience illustrates the dynamics and importance of the collaboration process.

Most schools are not as lucky as Cheltenham in having such a fine problem-solving program. In fact, many teachers report that they see students becoming more isolated all the time. A high school theatre director said recently, "Kids today don't socialize like we used to. They don't 'play' together. When I was a kid, we were always putting on shows and making up plays with puppets or people, so we could act all kinds of characters. It seems like the young people around today do everything by themselves. They like solitary activities like video games, watching television, or spending time in computer chat rooms. They seem to prefer virtual reality to actual reality! It's like pulling teeth to get them to audition for a show."

## COOPERATION FOR PROBLEM SOLVING

Before you start on these exercises for group problem solving, you might want to go back to Chapter 3, *Theatre Games to Promote Cooperation,* and ask your players to try the game *Tangle* again or review it. Remember what it took to untangle your circle, how many different solutions you tried, and how everyone was connected to everyone else. One person alone couldn't untangle the circle (solve the problem); it took everyone working together to make it happen. The same kind of cooperation is necessary in these problem-solving exercises. Make a point of involving multiethnic participants if possible.

The goal in these activities is to promote problem-solving skills while practicing cooperation to discover the best solution for the problem given. What's most important is the decision-making process that occurs before the action. Although one player is designated as the director, power sharing is necessary for genuine exploration of the problem. In other words, the solution isn't the director's alone; it must be the consensus of the group. The director may propose an answer, but the rest of the group must agree that this solution is the best one to solve the problem. This exercise offers the players the opportunity to use their knowledge and practice deductive skills in figuring out the solution.

The following improvisations offer specific puzzles to be solved by four actors. (Some group activities call for more where noted.) The whole class can prepare their improvisations at the same time, but let each group illustrate their solution one scene at a time. The trick with these situations is that there is no one best way. Possible solutions are included, based on what other student groups have come up with, but they are by no means the only answers to how these problems can be solved. With each of these dilemmas, give your players time to discuss the possible solutions among themselves. They will have to practice cooperation in listening to one another and decide on which solution they feel is best. The director in each group will coordinate the discussions. When each group appears to have a solution, ask them to act out their solution with dialogue. Remind them if their solution depends on characterization to add that element to their dialogue.

Since this work will move the players from simple improvisations to scene work, let's take a look at some acting tips before we begin.

Acting Tips for Scene Work

1. Actors listen to each other.
2. Actors look at each other.
3. Actors speak one at a time.
4. Actors don't walk when another actor is speaking.
5. Actors pick up their cues.
6. Actors don't interrupt each other.
7. Actors fill in for each other if someone goes blank.
8. Actors speak loud enough to be heard.
9. Actors focus on the moment.
10. Actors work together.

## COOPERATION WARM-UP

Direct your four-person team to assume the positions of a three-way mirror. The fourth person is the one trying on clothes. A three-way mirror has one image facing the person directly, another image on the right side and another on the left. Each mirror image sees the person from a slightly different angle. Suggest that the person stand directly in front of the center section first, then turn and face each side for a few moments. However, even when the person is facing center, the two side images still reflect a part of the person. Ask each of your players to take a turn as the person in the mirror. This will help your players tune in to each other and become aware of the other players' styles.

## PROBLEM-SOLVING SCENES

Divide the participants into groups of four or five actors in each scene. The first step for each group is to discuss the problem and brainstorm possible answers. When they have discussed the problem among themselves and come to an agreement on the best strategy for all concerned, they will improvise their solution with dialogue and perform for the rest of the assembly. If you have a particularly inhibited group or newcomers to drama, you may want to add a writing component to these problem situations. Ask your group to write out the script for their problem-solving scene with names for each of the players. Then ask them to read their script for the rest of the group if they are too self-conscious to improvise it. You can use the writing component with each of the problem-solving scenes. (Even some experienced actors are more comfortable with a script in hand.) Give your actors the option of improvising the scene after they have read their scripted version. Usually, after a group has scripted a few scenes, they are then ready to improvise.

### Problem #1: Rowboat

In this situation, two pairs are handcuffed to each other (two and two). They have been shipwrecked and their only chance for survival is to use a rowboat that one of the actors has discovered. The problem is that the boat will hold only three people. How do they save all four people? Each group must come up with their own ingenious method for survival under these circumstances. When they are ready, ask them to improvise their solution with dialogue.

(Possible solution: One handcuffed pair sits together and rows the boat with their uncuffed hands, while the other two are in the water and hold on to the back of the boat kicking their feet to help the boat move.)

### Problem #2: Avalanche

The class is divided into groups of five and told to imagine they are atop a mountain in a cabin. They have just heard on the radio that an avalanche is approaching. They have a toboggan with which to make their escape, but it seats only four. The group must find a solution for their dilemma that is agreeable to all.

This problem offers even more possibilities than the first one. Encourage the group to brainstorm ideas until they come to an agreement about which one they will choose. Again, ask them to illustrate their solution in an improvisation with dialogue.

(Possible solution: The fifth person sits on the lap of the first facing him, while the other three who are seated hold his legs up under their arms.)

## Problem #3: Hot air balloon

This group consists of four people who are in a hot air balloon above the ocean or other body of water. They discover a slow leak in the balloon. How do they save themselves and/or get back to solid ground?

(Possible solution: Check for any objects on the players, e.g., Band-Aid, chewing gum to patch the hole. If nothing, then one player stands on the shoulders of another, spits on his hand, and presses his hand tightly over the leak.)

## Problem #4: Elevator

Four people are stuck in an elevator between floors. Person Number One is a pregnant lady going into labor. The other three people have to figure out how to get the elevator moving or get help.

(Possible solution: After trying the emergency button, telephone, and banging on the elevator door, one person may stand on the shoulders of the other and go out the top emergency door and try to reach the floor above and open the door.

One high school senior came up with the idea of climbing up the side of the shaft to the next level where there is a release button to open the elevator doors.)

## Problem #5: Prison break-out

There are five people unjustly imprisoned for a political crime. Their eyes are blindfolded and hands are cuffed behind them. The guard is seated beside the door, which one actor (the leader) discovers is unlocked. The sound of snoring is heard coming from the guard. Apparently he is asleep. The problem is that the leader must round up the other four prisoners somehow and connect together to slip out the door silently without waking the guard. Players do not speak for fear of waking him.

(Possible solutions: The leader brings each player to him. He places one behind the other with himself in the lead and places each person's cuffed hands on the person in front of him. This is the way several blind people walk together, by placing a hand on the shoulder of the person in front of them. There are several variations on this, of course, but the necessary action is that each player is touching the one in front of him, who touches the one in front of her, until someone touches the leader. The additional problem in this exercise is that the players may not talk, so that creates an added burden of solving the problem in communicating without words.

## Problem # 6: Parachutes

Five people are on an airplane that is about to crash. There are four parachutes. What do they do? How do they solve their problem and do it quickly?

(Possible solution: Two people might tie themselves together or both hold on tightly to each other with one of them wearing the parachute. Since it was not stated that the people are adults, two of the people might be children, and one parachute could be put on both of them.)

## Problem # 7: Rocket ship

This problem is different from the others in that it is creative rather than reactive. Again there are five actors in this group. These players must decide who each of the five people are and which of them will be sent on the first rocket ship to Mars. These travelers are passengers, not the pilot or crew. The actors must create characters other than themselves for these roles. (In other words, one can't play a sixteen-year-old high school student if he really is one.) Who are they? What is the profession of each? How old are they? What is their gender? What kind of personalities do they have? (For example, one character may be a fifty-year-old woman rocket scientist who hates the world on Earth and wants to leave it) The group must create the five characters who will take the trip and all must agree that each character is an asset to the whole group. Give them plenty of time for discussion with this one. When they are in agreement about the five characters, each actor selects one to portray and introduces himself or herself as that character. When the introductions are over, ask for discussion on how the choices were made. Is the whole group in agreement with the selections? Does another member of the class have an idea for a different person who was overlooked? Would any of the players be willing to change characters for one offered by the class? Ask each group to explain how they practiced cooperation in this exercise.

The following exercises deal with character problems rather than situations. The preparations involve simply deciding who the characters are and beginning the scene immediately, so that the audience hears all of the discussion in the decision. The problems here will evolve from the kind of characters the actors choose to play. As you will see, once again there are no simple solutions. The resolution will depend on how the characters see the situation.

## Problem #8: "No comprendo"

There is only one person in this scene who speaks English. The three other players are of a different race and culture and speak no English. Ask them to speak in gibberish (no known language but just made-up sounds and words. If this proves too difficult, use numbers. They can be any numbers and don't have to be in any particular order.) These people ask directions to get to a place that is important to them. The three people will decide where that place is but cannot tell the fourth person. The improvisation will begin here.

The fourth person will try to understand where the other three want to go and give them directions on how to get there—if he can. For example, they may need to get to a hospital, a police department, an airport, a famous tourist attraction, and so on. Stop the scene when the fourth person succeeds in understanding where they want to go and gives directions, or when the frustration level becomes too high.

The next three problems also have no simple solutions. They offer the players the opportunity to make an educated guess, solve an ethical dilemma, or come up with a moral decision. Again, these situations are meant for improvisation, but feel free to use them for a playwriting exercise as well.

## Problem # 9: Sinking ship

You are on a sinking ship. There is a lifeboat ready to go, but there is a storm and the ocean waves are so high they will probably capsize the lifeboat. Do you try the lifeboat or stay on the sinking ship? You are five close friends who want to stay together. (Sternberg 1982)

(There is no easy answer on this or the next one)

## Problem # 10: Mountain cabin

You are in a mountain cabin with your guide and three friends (five players). Your guide has a broken leg and must remain immobile. Friend Number One is ill with all the symptoms of appendicitis and needs immediate medical attention. Although an avalanche is predicted, you have a toboggan. What do you do? Who goes? Who stays? How do you get help?

## Problem # 11: Mountain climbing

You are in a mountain-climbing accident. Five people are tied on a rope. The last person has fallen in a ravine and is unconscious and unseen, so we don't need an actor to play this role. The second-to-last one is in a precarious position and may fall. What do you do? Do you try to rescue the unseen Number Five? Do you cut the rope between Number Four and Number Five? The four players must decide.

## Problem #12: Physical problems—Raft

This is a simple physical problem of space and balance. You are on a raft in shark-infested waters. (Your raft is a board approximately three feet by three feet, marked out on the floor.) Five people have to stand on board and balance themselves for thirty seconds.

## Problem #13: Pyramid

Most players will remember the five-person pyramid with three people on the bottom, two on top of them, and one on top of them. This variation asks for the same kind of pyramid but using six participants in such a way that each one is an integral part of the structure.

## SUMMARY

Working together in a cooperative setting is what theatre is all about. Theatre creates dramatic life experiences that run the gamut of human emotions. It teaches us ways to solve problems and/or behave in a crisis situation without the fear of consequences. The goal in these activities is to promote problem-solving skills while practicing cooperation to discover the best solution for a problem. What's most important is the decision-making process that occurs before the action. These exercises offer players the opportunity to use their knowledge and practice deductive skills in figuring out solutions to the problems. Communication among the players and the director is vital for a successful performance. Studies reviewed indicate that cooperation in multiethnic groups is one of the most effective ways to help students attain more positive racial attitudes.

# 9

# POV-Doubling Scenes

The real voyage of discovery consists not in seeing new
landscapes but in having new eyes.

*Marcel Proust*

The term P.O.V., which means point of view, is used in filmmaking.
It means that the camera shoots from a certain point of view (when
spoken, the letters are read separately—P-O-V). It can be from one of
the character's perspectives, for example, how he or she sees the
other people or things in the room. It's as if the camera is looking
at the scene through the eyes of a specific character. If Rose is
looking at Tony, the camera pans in for a close-up on Tony's angry
face as he looks at her. We see Tony's face because the scene is being
shot from Rose's P.O.V. It shows how she sees Tony's angry face. If
we see a shot of Rose's surprised face, the shot is from Tony's P.O.V.

Psychodrama and sociodrama use a technique called "*the double.*"
When a person doubles for another, he or she expresses that person's unexpressed thoughts and feelings.

Many things go through our minds that we don't voice aloud. In
exploring social interactions, Jacob L. Moreno, the creator of both
psychodrama and sociodrama, believed that it was valuable to hear
what people were thinking and feeling so that what was normally
hidden in a situation became manifest. He invented a special role to
bring hidden process to the surface (Moreno 1975, 240). "That role,
*the double*, is played by one or more group members. The double is
a mind/feeling reader. He or she is a person whose role it is to tune
into the enactor's hidden voice, one's truest self. The double helps

the enactor realize and acknowledge what she is thinking and feeling" (Sternberg and Garcia 1989, 59).

For example, let's give Rose a double when she looks at Tony. Rose's double says what she's thinking, "There he goes exploding again. Everything I say makes him angry. What's wrong with him?"

Tony does not respond to the double, since that is Rose's inner voice and Tony doesn't hear it. Based on those inner thoughts, Rose might now say, "What's really bothering you, Tony?"

The double supports with statements that affirm the actor, validating thoughts, feelings, opinions, and actions. There is a scene in the play *Androcles and the Lion*, adapted by the playwright Aurand Harris (1964), in which Androcles meets the Lion. Each character speaks his underlying thoughts to the audience as an aside, complete with his particular prejudice against the other.

ANDROCLES: He's going to eat me.
LION: He's going to beat me.

Then each steps back in the scene returning to the reality of the character in the scene. If these asides were done by a person other than the characters themselves, it would be a POV- double.

For the work in this chapter these two techniques, the POV and the double, are combined. In the following scenes, you will see examples of the POV-double from all three characters' perspectives. This first scene selected is a partial one, from Shakespeare's *Romeo and Juliet*, and will illustrate how this can be done. This play is a good example of *past grievances* as a classic cause of conflict. Read the scene through first just as it is written and ask your players to think of what the inner voice double of each of the characters might be thinking and/or feeling.

## ROMEO AND JULIET
**CHARACTERS**
Act III, scene v *Romeo and Juliet are at her window.*
   (*Enter Nurse, hastily*)

NURSE: Madam!
JULIET: Nurse?
NURSE: Your lady mother's coming to your chamber.
   The day is broke, be wary, look about.
   (*Exit*)

JULIET: Then window, let day in and let life out.
ROMEO: Farewell, farewell! One kiss, and I'll descend.
   (*He goeth down*)
JULIET: Art thou gone so, love? Lord, my husband, friend,
   I must hear from thee every day i'th' hour,
   For in a minute there are many days—
   O by this count I shall be much in years
   Ere I again behold my Romeo.
ROMEO: Farewell.
   I will omit no opportunity
   That may convey my greetings, love, to thee.
JULIET: O think'st thou we shall ever meet again?
ROMEO: Ay, doubt it not, and all these woes shall serve
   For sweet discourses in our times to come.
JULIET: O God! I have an ill-divining soul,
   Methinks I see thee, now thou art so low,
   As one dead in the bottom of a tomb.
   Either my eyesight fails or thou look'st pale.
ROMEO: And trust me, love, in my eye so do you—
   Dry Sorrow drinks our blood. Adieu, adieu! (*Exit*)
JULIET: O Fortune, Fortune! All men call thee fickle.
   If thou art fickle, what doest thou with him
   That is renown'd for faith? Be fickle, Fortune,
   For then I hope thou wilt not keep him long
   But send him back—
      (*Enter Lady Capulet*)

After each of the POV-double roles, discuss what the double felt after each scene. Ask the characters they double for if their double captured what they were feeling. Did the characters feel anything different from what their double said at any given time? This is an important part of the work and should be repeated after each scene.

   Let's begin our POV-double with the nurse. What is she thinking and/or feeling when she enters the scene? It might be something like this:

Act III, scene v *Romeo and Juliet are at her window.*
**POV-DOUBLE FOR NURSE**
(*Enter Nurse, hastily*)

   **POV-DOUBLE: Hey, kid, you're in trouble.**
   NURSE: Madam!

JULIET: Nurse?

**POV-DOUBLE**: **You'd better get that guy out of your bedroom fast before your mother catches you. It's morning already.**

NURSE: Your lady mother's coming to your chamber.
The day is broke, be wary, look about.

**POV-DOUBLE**: **I'd better get out of here myself before her old lady thinks I'm in on it.**
*(Exit)*

JULIET: Then window, let day in and let life out.

ROMEO: Farewell, farewell! One kiss, and I'll descend.
*(He goeth down)*

JULIET: Art thou gone so, love? Lord, my husband, friend,
I must hear from thee every day i'th' hour,
For in a minute there are many days—
O by this count I shall be much in years
Ere I again behold my Romeo.

ROMEO: Farewell.
I will omit no opportunity
That may convey my greetings, love, to thee.

JULIET: O think'st thou we shall ever meet again?

ROMEO: Ay,doubt it not, and all these woes shall serve
For sweet discourses in our times to come.

JULIET: O God! I have an ill-divining soul,
Methinks I see thee, now thou art so low,
As one dead in the bottom of a tomb.
Either my eyesight fails or thou look'st pale.

ROMEO: And trust me, love, in my eye so do you—
Dry Sorrow drinks our blood. Adieu, adieu!     *(Exit)*

JULIET: O Fortune, Fortune! All men call thee fickle.
If thou art fickle, what doest thou with him
That is renown'd for faith? Be fickle, Fortune,
For then I hope thou wilt not keep him long
But send him back—
*(Enter Lady Capulet)*

Now, let's try Romeo and see what he's thinking or feeling. Remember you don't have to have a double before every line. Sometimes we speak our inner thoughts exactly the way we're thinking.

Act III, scene v *Romeo and Juliet are at her window.*
**POV-DOUBLE FOR ROMEO**
*(Enter Nurse, hastily)*

NURSE: Madam!

JULIET: Nurse?

NURSE: Your lady mother's coming to your chamber.
   The day is broke, be wary, look about.
   (*Exit*)

JULIET: Then window, let day in and let life out.

**POV-DOUBLE: Oh, baby, I don't want to leave you.**

ROMEO: Farewell, farewell! One kiss, and I'll descend.
   (*He goeth down*)

JULIET: Art thou gone so, love? Lord, my husband, friend,
   I must hear from thee every day i'th' hour,
   For in a minute there are many days—
   O by this count I shall be much in years
   Ere I again behold my Romeo.

**POV-DOUBLE: I'd better get out of here while I can, but I'll be
back and thinking of you every minute.**

ROMEO: Farewell.
   I will omit no opportunity
   That may convey my greetings, love, to thee.

JULIET: O think'st thou we shall ever meet again?

**POV-DOUBLE: You can bet on it. Someday we'll look back on all
this and laugh about it.**

ROMEO: Ay, doubt it not, and all these woes shall serve
   For sweet discourses in our times to come.

JULIET: O God! I have an ill-divining soul,
   Methinks I see thee, now thou art so low,
   As one dead in the bottom of a tomb.
   Either my eyesight fails or thou look'st pale.

ROMEO: And trust me, love, in my eye so do you—

**POV-DOUBLE: We're just tired but we'll be fine. Never fear.**

   Dry Sorrow drinks our blood. Adieu, adieu! (*Exit*)

JULIET: O Fortune, Fortune! All men call thee fickle.
   If thou art fickle, what doest thou with him
   That is renown'd for faith? Be fickle, Fortune,
   For then I hope thou wilt not keep him long
   But send him back—
      (*Enter Lady Capulet*)

Now it's Juliet's turn. What might she be thinking/feeling inside
while all this action is going on? She has the most to lose in this
scene, of course, but then she's in love and that makes a difference

in how one looks at things. Select one of your players to do the POV-double for Juliet. Suggested places for the insert are marked in the script, but this time the POV-double player improvises her own lines.

Act III, scene v *Romeo and Juliet are at her window.*
**POV-double FOR JULIET**
(*Enter Nurse, hastily*)

NURSE: Madam!
JULIET: Nurse?
NURSE: Your lady mother's coming to your chamber.
   The day is broke, be wary, look about.
   (*Exit*)
**POV-double:** _____
JULIET: Then window, let day in and let life out.
ROMEO: Farewell, farewell! One kiss, and I'll descend.
   (*He goeth down*)
**POV-double:** _____
JULIET: Art thou gone so, love? Lord, my husband, friend,
   I must hear from thee every day i'th' hour,
   For in a minute there are many days—
   O by this count I shall be much in years
   Ere I again behold my Romeo.
ROMEO: Farewell.
   I will omit no opportunity
   That may convey my greetings, love, to thee.
**POV-double:** _____
JULIET: O think'st thou we shall ever meet again?
ROMEO: Ay, doubt it not, and all these woes shall serve
   For sweet discourses in our times to come.
**POV-double::** _____
JULIET: O God! I have an ill-divining soul,
   Methinks I see thee, now thou art so low,
   As one dead in the bottom of a tomb.
   Either my eyesight fails or thou look'st pale.
ROMEO: And trust me, love, in my eye so do you—
   Dry Sorrow drinks our blood. Adieu, adieu!   (*Exit*)
JULIET: O Fortune, Fortune! All men call thee fickle.
   If thou art fickle, what doest thou with him
   That is renown'd for faith? Be fickle, Fortune,

> For then I hope thou wilt not keep him long
> But send him back—
> > (*Enter Lady Capulet*)

As you can see there is a certain similarity to what actors call *subtext* to this technique. Subtext is defined by Felner in her book, *Free to Act* (1989, 114) as "the internal images that determine the significance of your words and reveal your inner objective, what you really want at a given moment." However, subtext requires that the inner thoughts be created on the basis of the given circumstances in the script. In our POV-double technique our inner thoughts may never be verbalized but remain with us only as hidden feelings which may or may not affect the way the line is spoken.

This POV-doubling technique is exceptionally useful in dealing with conflict resolution scenes. Take a look at the scenes below, which deal with common interpersonal conflicts. Select your players and ask them to do the POV-double as the character they choose to play in the scene. Use one POV-double each time the scene is played.

You can see how you could use this technique with any of Shakespeare's plays or any other you might use for study in literature.

"I finally got my kids' attention reading Shakespeare when I used the POV-double technique with them. They got a real kick out of trying to figure out what the characters were really thinking that they didn't say. Some of their ideas were pretty far out, but at least they had some ideas! It got them started and that's what counts," commented an Ohio high school teacher.

The next scene is one between a mother and daughter, with a slightly unusual twist to the mother/daughter conflict. Family conflicts have inspired playwrights from the Greeks on down to today's soap operas. Remember *Medea*? Although this conflict is less violent, the play, *Mrs. Warren's Profession* by George Bernard Shaw, caused quite a stir when it was first written in 1894, for Mrs. Warren's profession was shocking and socially unacceptable. She was the madam of a high-class brothel. Although the play seems pretty tame to us today, *Mrs. Warren's Profession* was banned and its performance prohibited. Critics of the period labeled it as "immoral and otherwise improper for the stage." It wasn't until eight years later that the play was performed by the private Stage Society. How times have changed! The scene is cut to eliminate the need for exposition.

## MRS. WARREN'S PROFESSION

### CHARACTERS

Mrs. Warren Middle-aged, formerly pretty. Rather spoiled and domineering, genial, former madam. Mother of Vivie.

Vivie Attractive specimen of the sensible, able, highly educated young woman. Age early twenties. Strong, confident, and self-possessed.

Act II

MRS. WARREN: What nonsense is this you're trying to talk? Do you want to show your independence, now that you're a great little person at school? Don't be a fool, child.

VIVIE (*Indulgently*): That's all you have to say on the subject, is it, mother?

MRS. WARREN (*Puzzled, then angry*): Don't you keep asking me questions like that. (*Violently*) Hold your tongue. You and your way of life, indeed! What next? (*She looks at Vivie again. No reply.*) Your way of life will be what I please, so it will. (*Another pause.*) I've been noticing these airs in you ever since you got that tripos or whatever you call it. If you think I'm going to put up with them you're mistaken; and the sooner you find it out the better. (*Muttering*) All I have to say on the subject, indeed! (*Again raising her voice angrily*) Do you know who you're speaking to, Miss?

VIVIE (*Looking across at her without raising her head from her book*): No. Who are you? What are you?

MRS. WARREN (*Rising breathless*): You young imp!

VIVIE: Everybody knows my reputation, my social standing, and the profession I intend to pursue. I know nothing about you. What is the way of life which you invite me to share with you and Sir George Crofts, pray?

MRS. WARREN: Take care. I shall do something I'll be sorry for after, and you too.

VIVIE (*Putting aside her books with cool decision*): Well, let us drop the subject until you are better able to face it. (*Looking critically at her mother*)

MRS. WARREN (*Piteously*): Oh, my darling, how can you be so hard on me? Have I no rights over you as your mother?

VIVIE: Are you my mother?

MRS. WARREN (*Appalled*): Am I your mother! Oh, Vivie!

VIVIE: Then where are our relatives? My father? Our family friends? You claim the rights of a mother; the right to call me fool and child; to speak to me as no woman in authority over me at college dare speak to me; to dictate my way of life; and to force on me the acquaintance of a brute whom anyone can see to be the most vicious sort of London man about town. Before I give myself the trouble to resist such claims, I may as well find out whether they have any real existence.

MRS. WARREN (*Distracted, throwing herself on her knees*): Oh, no, no. Stop, stop. I am your mother; I swear it. Oh, you can't mean to turn on me—my own child! It's not natural. You believe me, don't you? Say you believe me.

VIVIE: Who was my father?

MRS. WARREN: You don't know what you're asking. I can't tell you.

VIVIE (*Determinedly*): Oh, yes, you can, if you like. I have a right to know and you know very well that I have that right. You can refuse to tell me, if you please; but if you do, you will see the last of me tomorrow morning.

MRS. WARREN: Oh, it's too horrible to hear you talk like that. You wouldn't—you couldn't leave me.

VIVIE (*Ruthlessly*): Yes, without a moment's hesitation, if you trifle with me about this.

The character in this scene who is hiding her feelings is Mrs. Warren, of course. She may be thinking one thing and saying another. Vivie seems pretty straightforward and says what she's thinking. Possible POV-double spots are marked in the next script with suggestions for the dialogue.

## MRS. WARREN'S PROFESSION

### Act II

MRS. WARREN: What nonsense is this you're trying to talk? Do you want to show your independence, now that you're a great little person at school? Don't be a fool, child.

VIVIE (*Indulgently*): That's all you have to say on the subject, is it, mother?

**POV-**<small>DOUBLE</small> **FOR MRS. WARREN**: **How dare she question me? Who does she think she is? I'll have to take her down a peg or two.**

M<small>RS</small>. W<small>ARREN</small> (*Puzzled, then angry*): Don't you keep asking me questions like that. (*Violently*) Hold your tongue. You and your way of life, indeed! What next? (*She looks at Vivie again. No reply.*) Your way of life will be what I please, so it will. (*Another pause*) I've been noticing these airs in you ever since you got that tripos or whatever you call it. If you think I'm going to put up with them you're mistaken; and the sooner you find it out the better. (*Muttering*) All I have to say on the subject, indeed! (*Again raising her voice angrily*) Do you know who you're speaking to, Miss?

V<small>IVIE</small> (*Looking across at her without raising her head from her book*): No. Who are you? What are you?

**POV-**<small>DOUBLE</small>: **Is she questioning my integrity?**

M<small>RS</small>. W<small>ARREN</small> (*Rising breathless*): You young imp!

V<small>IVIE</small>: Everybody knows my reputation, my social standing, and the profession I intend to pursue. I know nothing about you. What is the way of life which you invite me to share with you and Sir George Crafts, pray?

M<small>RS</small>. W<small>ARREN</small>: Take care. I shall do something I'll be sorry for after, and you too.

V<small>IVIE</small> (*Putting aside her books with cool decision*): Well, let us drop the subject until you are better able to face it. (*Looking critically at her mother*)

**POV-**<small>DOUBLE</small>: **Poor me! Poor me!**

M<small>RS</small>. W<small>ARREN</small> (*Piteously*): Oh, my darling, how can you be so hard on me? Have I no rights over you as your mother?

V<small>IVIE</small>: Are you my mother?

M<small>RS</small>. W<small>ARREN</small> (*Appalled*): Am I your mother! Oh, Vivie!

V<small>IVIE</small>: Then where are our relatives? My father? Our family friends? You claim the rights of a mother; the right to call me fool and child; to speak to me as no woman in authority over me at college dare speak to me; to dictate my way of life; and to force on me the acquaintance of a brute whom anyone can see to be the most vicious sort of London man about town. Before I give myself the trouble to resist such claims, I may as well find out whether they have any real existence.

**POV-**<small>DOUBLE</small>: **Oh, oh! What's she doing to me? I have to make her believe me.**

MRS. WARREN (*Distracted, throwing herself on her knees*): Oh, no, no. Stop, stop. I am your mother; I swear it. Oh, you can't mean to turn on me—my own child! It's not natural. You believe me, don't you? Say you believe me.

VIVIE: Who was my father?

**POV-DOUBLE: I was afraid that was coming. I can't tell her.**

MRS. WARREN: You don't know what you're asking. I can't tell you.

VIVIE (*Determinedly*): Oh, yes, you can, if you like. I have a right to know and you know very well that I have that right. You can refuse to tell me, if you please; but if you do, you will see the last of me tomorrow morning.

**POV-DOUBLE: She doesn't mean it. She can't.**

MRS. WARREN: Oh, it's too horrible to hear you talk like that. You wouldn't—you couldn't leave me.

VIVIE (*Ruthlessly*): Yes, without a moment's hesitation, if you trifle with me about this.

Other players may have different feelings from those expressed in the POV-double dialogue inserted above and/or may want to double at other spots. Try the scene again using the first script and offer different players the opportunity to double for Mrs. Warren's role. Some of your participants may be eager to try Vivie's POV-double as well. Give those actors a chance to double for Vivie, adding their voices wherever they feel it might be useful.

Don't forget to discuss feelings of the double after each scene and ask the actors playing the characters if they felt their doubles captured what they were feeling at the time. This discussion will very often pinpoint the origin of conflict. Remind your players to take note of the three sources of conflict: challenges to ego or respect, or rekindling of past grievances. As you can see, all three are found in the previous scene.

Here is a list of plays that include conflict situation scenes for children, adolescents, and young adults and that work well using the POV-double technique. This list is highly subjective and offers these selections for no reason other than that they are some of the author's favorites.

| | |
|---|---|
| *Ah, Wilderness!* | Eugene O'Neill |
| *Our Town* | Thorton Wilder |
| *A Raisin in the Sun* | Lorraine Hansberry |

| | |
|---|---|
| *The Wild Duck* | Henrik Ibsen |
| *The Master Builder* | ———— |
| *The Children's Hour* | Lillian Hellman |
| *Picnic* | William Inge |
| *The Crucible* | Arthur Miller |
| *Death of a Salesman* | |
| *The Glass Menagerie* | ———— |
| *Member of the Wedding* | Tennessee Williams |
| *The Grass Harp* | Carson McCullers |
| *The Importance of Being Earnest* | Truman Capote |
| *Agnes of God* | Oscar Wilde |
| *Dutchman* | John Pielmeier |
| *'Night, Mother* | Amiri Baraka |
| *Tea and Sympathy* | Marsha Norman |
| *Master Harold and the Boys* | Robert Anderson |
| *Thousand Clowns* | Athol Fugard |
| *Miracle Worker* | Herb Gardner |
| *Vanities* | William Gibson |
| *To Kill a Mockingbird* | Jack Heffner |
| *For Colored Girls* | Harper Lee |
| *Barefoot in the Park* | Ntozake Shange |
| *Brighton Beach Memoirs* | Neil Simon |
| *Fences* | ———— |
| | August Wilson |

If you are a theatre teacher, director, or just a plain theatre buff, you are probably familiar with many of these plays. Select one that you know and pick a scene from it. Give your players a brief outline of the story and a character description of the roles in the scene you chose. For example, one of the author's all-time favorites is *Member of the Wedding* by Carson McCullers. Frankie, a twelve-year-old girl, is the main character, and most adolescents can identify with her problems. The play is about her coming of age. She is a lonely, awkward, hot-tempered and highly imaginative ugly duckling who feels the world should take notice of her. She longs for companionship, as do many young people at this stage in their lives. Frankie's mother is dead and her father pays little attention to her. This situation fits only too well the single parent profile of many families of young people today. Frankie spends her time mostly with the good-natured cook Bernice Sadie Brown and her seven-year-old cousin, John Henry. There are some other minor female characters slightly older than Frankie who add to her unhappiness when they refuse to elect her into their club. In her frustration she decides to accompany her brother Jarvis and his bride on their honeymoon. That scene with her brother would serve well as a POV-double both from Frankie's POV and her brother's. Frankie is heartbroken when the couple leave without her. Three months later, Frankie has passed through one of life's big transitions and has become Frances, to whom the thirteen-year-old football husky next door appears to be a Greek god.

There are several scenes which work well for the POV-double technique. In fact, any in which Frankie appears offers some conflict. Once again, remember to discuss the feelings of the players, both characters and POV-doubles, after each playing.

The next scene is a scripted one and has three very distinct POVs. In fact, this scene shows us each of the characters in conflict with each of the others. Try this scene in the same way. Read it through once as it is. Then play it again with a POV-double for Joey, for Mr. S, and for Jake.

## THE PIZZA PARLOR (Sternberg 1982)

### CHARACTERS

Joey  About sixteen, friendly, nice kid

Mr. S.  Elderly owner of the pizza parlor, gruff exterior but likes kids and is especially fond of Joey

Jake Jaretti  Slick, menacing, interested only in money and doesn't care how he gets it

*The scene is set at the counter of a pizza parlor. Mr. S., the old man, is behind the counter and Joey is seated at the counter.*

MR. S.: That's $3.85. (*Puts check down in front of Joey*)

JOEY (*Going through his pockets*): Eh . . . her . . . hey. Mr. S., it looks like I've got a problem.

MR. S. (*Wearily*): You and the rest of the world, Joey.

JOEY: I mean—I—I've got an immediate problem.

MR. S.: What's your problem?

JOEY: I must have left my wallet in my locker.

MR. S.: Oh, you kids are all alike—always giving me trouble.

JOEY: Aw, come on, Mr. S. I never gave you any trouble. I'll pay you tomorrow, I promise. I have to go or I'll be late for practice.

MR. S.: Tomorrow . . . tomorrow. It's always tomorrow. Well, I got news for you kids. Maybe I won't be here tomorrow.

JOEY: What do you mean?

MR. S.: I'm sellin' this dump. I'm sick and tired of it. I've had it with all you kids.

JOEY: You're kidding. (*Pause*) You wouldn't sell this place.

MR. S.: Oh, yeah?—Just watch me. Mr. Jaretti will be here in about ten minutes to finalize the deal.

JOEY: Jake Jaretti?

MR. S.: (*Surprised*) Yeah, how do you know him?

JOEY: He's got a reputation.

MR. S.: People talk.

JOEY: I know he sells dope to kids. I know that. He hangs around my brother's school.

MR. S.: Nah, you're mistaken.

(*Jake Jaretti enters unnoticed by the other two. He stands at the door listening.*)

JOEY: No, I'm not, Mr. S. You can't sell the pizza parlor to him. You just can't.

MR. S.: I already made the deal.

JOEY: Don't do it.

JAKE: Hey, kid, nobody asked you for advice.

(*Joey and Mr. S. turn and look at him*)

MR. S.: Hello, Mr. Jaretti, we didn't notice you come in.

JAKE: Beat it, kid.

MR. S.: He's all right.

JAKE: I said "beat it." We got business to discuss.

MR. S.: Listen, Mr. Jaretti, I need some more time to think about this.

JAKE: You're out of time, old man.

JOEY: Don't do anything you'll be sorry for, Mr. S.

JAKE: Kid, what's the matter? You deaf? I said, "Get out!"

MR. S.: It's all right, Joey. Go ahead. You're already late for practice.

(*Joey gets up and hesitates*)

JAKE (*Starts toward him menacingly*): I said *leave*. I mean "Now!"

(*Joey leaves*)

You can see how one conflict leads into another in this scene. Play a POV-double for each of the characters, and play it several times or as many times as different participants want to act a specific role.

Joey is the one with the most ambivalence, of course. Once again, facilitate the group to discuss their feelings after playing a POV-double, a role, or just watching the action. What were some of the feelings the audience had while watching the scene?

You can use this technique with any literature. It doesn't have to be a play. Try it with a scene from a novel or short story. There may be other opportunities that arise in different subject areas. Keep the technique in mind to use whenever you feel it might be appropriate to uncover the underlying feelings in a situation.

## SUMMARY

The POV-double technique combines methods used in other disciplines, both film and psychodrama/sociodrama. The POV-double is a way to explore unexpressed thoughts and feelings. The person in this role affirms the actor's thoughts, feelings, opinions, and actions to help the player realize and acknowledge them. The POV-double tunes into one character's point of view (POV). This experience helps us to understand where a conflict begins and how it can escalate. It allows us to say the things that are normally thought but left unsaid. It offers the players the opportunity not only to put themselves in another person's shoes but also to explore unstated feelings. The importance of discussion after the scene cannot be stressed enough. It is vital that the players, as well as the audience, get the opportunity to talk about what they felt as they played the scene, as well as when they viewed it. What were the conflicts? How were the conflicts brought out or buried within? In the discussion, remember there are no right or wrong responses when you are dealing with feelings. Respect whatever your participants are willing to give. This technique can be used to explore any literature as well as other subject areas.

# 10

# Monologues to Explore Feelings

This above all: To thine own self be true,
And it must follow as the night the day,
Thou canst not then be false to any man."

*Shakespeare*

Who are you? What do you want to say? What are you feeling? We all have an inner voice that speaks to us, but we are not always able to heed it. Often we ignore it, or tell it, "I don't want to hear you," or "Nobody else thinks that way. I can't be the only one!" We shut down our inner voice, squelch it before it has a chance to influence us. We certainly won't allow it to become our outer voice, because then people would know how we feel, and what we need and think.

Yet, we long to find our voice, to be able to say, "I want that," or "That doesn't feel right to me," or just plain "no." Those who have freed their inner voice are more able to express their thoughts, their needs, and their feelings. They are equipped to meet conflict and explore ways to resolve it. If we can help our players find a voice, we can help them express their needs. When we are able to express our needs, we can make informed choices, and more choices also become available to us. The person who is psychologically healthy is in touch with the self. She is aware of her feelings and attitudes, values and beliefs. She is more in communication with herself than is the psychologically unhealthy person. Actors speak of "finding their voice" or "discovering the voice of the character." One of the ways we can help participants find their voice and use it is through the *monologue*. The monologue has been around as long as the theatre and serves many uses in drama.

In theatre terms a monologue is one actor on the stage speaking to another who is unseen, or it can be the actor speaking to the audience as that character. A monologue can be created by cutting the second actor's lines and the first actor simply responding as if the second one spoke to him. A soliloquy, on the other hand, is the actor speaking his thoughts. For example, Hamlet's famous speech below is actually a dramatic soliloquy, which is how the dictionary defines a monologue—"a dramatic soliloquy." For our purposes then, we will refer to the monologue as any one person speech, whether the actor is speaking to another unseen character, the audience, or his inner thoughts.

Let's take a look at the famous well known monologue, which is definitely dealing with the actor's inner thoughts.

## HAMLET

ACT III, Scene I

*(Enter Hamlet)*

HAMLET: To be or not to be, that is the question:
   Whether 'tis nobler in the mind to suffer
   The slings and arrows of outrageous fortune,
   Or to take arms against a sea of troubles
   And by opposing end them. To die: to sleep.
   No more; and by a sleep to say we end
   The heartache and the thousand natural shocks
   That flesh is heir to: 'tis a consummation
   Devoutly to be wished. To die: to sleep
   To sleep: perchance to dream. Ay, there's the rub;
   For in that sleep of death what dreams may come
   When we have shuffled off this mortal coil
   Must give us pause. There's the respect
   That makes calamity of so long life;
   For who would bear the whips and scorns of time,
   Th' oppressor's wrong, the proud man's contumely,
   The pangs of despised love, the law's delay,
   The insolence of office, and the spurns
   That patient merit of th' unworthy takes,
   When he himself might his quietus make
   With a bare bodkin? Who would fardels bear.
   To grunt and sweat under a weary life

But that the dread of something after death,
The undiscover'd country from whose bourn
No traveler returns, puzzles the will,
And makes us rather bear those ills we have
Than fly to others that we know not of?
Thus conscience does make cowards of us all,
And thus the native hue of resolution
Is sicklied o' with pale cast of thought,
And enterprises of great pitch and moment
With this regard their currents turn awry,
And lose the name of action.—Soft you now!
The fair Ophelia! Nymph, in thy orisons
Be all my sins remember'd.

Although most of us don't speak in iambic pentameter, we do talk to ourselves now and then. Some actors do it all the time as a way to help them get into character. Others weigh and balance a decision or resolve a conflict by voicing both sides of an issue.

The next monologue is an example of the actor speaking to the audience as if they were another character or characters in the play. This is a famous monologue spoken by Sojourner Truth, the black slave from the state of New York who was received in the marble halls of Congress by no less than three different presidents. She fought for the rights of all humankind, as she states in a line from the play, *Sojourner* (Sternberg and Beechman 1989, 30–31)

I'm not agitatin' for colored folks' rights or women's rights,
I'm agitatin' for *human rights!*

The short monologue below is known as the "Ain't I a Woman" speech, which Sojourner gave at a Women's Rights Convention in Akron, Ohio, in 1852.

### Sojourner

SOJOURNER: Well, children, where there is so much racket there must be something out of kilter. I think between the colored folks of the south and the women of the north—all talkin' about rights—the white men will be in a pretty fix soon.
That man over there—
(*She points to the second reverend*)

He says women need to be helped into carriages and lifted over ditches and to have the best everywhere.

(*She smiles and shakes her head negatively*)
   Nobody ever helped me into carriages, over mud puddles or gets me the best places. Ain't I a woman? Look at me.

(*She pulls up her sleeve to display her muscular arm and holds it up high*)
   Look at my arm. I have plowed, and I have planted. And, I have gathered into barns. And no man could head me.— And, ain't I a woman? I could work as much and eat as much as any man—(*after thought*) . . . when I could get it. And bear the lash as well. (*Her voice rising*) And, ain't I a woman? I have borne children and none but Jesus heard me. And, ain't I a woman?

(*She looks over at the first reverend and points to him*)
   He talks about this thing in the head.

(*She hesitates and looks to the woman nearest her*)
   What's that they call it? (*Nods approvingly*) Intellect. That's it, honey.

(*Turns her attention back to the audience*)
   What's that got to do with women's rights or colored folks' rights? If my cup won't hold but a pint, and yours holds a quart, wouldn't you be mean not to let me have my little half measure full?
   (*Pointing to the second reverend*) That little man in black there, he says women can't have as much rights as men, 'cause Christ wasn't a woman.
   (*Her arms outstretched*) Where did Christ come from?
(*She looks directly at him.*)
   From God and a woman. Man had nothing to do with him.

(*Sojourner smiles knowing she has made her point. Now She turns her attention back to the women in the audience.*)
   If the first woman God ever made was strong enough to turn the world upside down all alone, these women to-gether ought to be able to turn it back and get it right side up again. Now that they are asking to do it, the men better let 'em . . . And, now old Sojourner has nothing more to say.

(*She stoops over and picks up her bonnet from the table. She carries it in her hand.*)
   Obliged to you for hearing me.

Monologues serve a variety of purposes in the theatre and are a favorite device to create historical characters portrayed in the time period. They offer a dramatic method to provide exposition in a personal, intense way.

## HISTORICAL PERSPECTIVES

Actually the monologue above is a good example of a historical perspective monologue. It deals with a famous woman in American history. The monologue is a good format through which to develop basic understanding of historical events and personalities. A great deal of research is necessary to write a historical monologue. You put yourself in the character's shoes. You have to not only know the famous speeches or writings of the character, but also acquire enough information about the period and the person to make him come alive, to make what he says seem real. You must know the conflicts the character faced and how he resolved them. In other words, the actor must try to understand the feelings behind the words. Using the lives of heroes and heroines provides a framework for the group to develop basic understanding of a period in history. It offers your players insight into the times and illustrates the fact that the human condition does not change much.

   The key to creating a believable monologue is to create a living, breathing, human being that you can identify with, someone you really know and understand. That doesn't mean that you have to like the character in your monologue, but you do have to understand how that person participated in the events of his or her time.

   Creating a historical monologue is particularly effective for anyone who views history as dry and boring, or as one student named Dave put it, "Who cares about a lot of dead dudes who died a hundred years ago?"

   He changed his mind after he picked a famous line to research for his monologue. Dave chose the line "Give me liberty or give me death." He discovered there was more to this speech than those famous words of Patrick Henry.

   "That dude really understood freedom. He made this speech at the Virginia Convention in Richmond, Virginia, on March 23,

1775. That's over two hundred years ago," Dave stated proudly, pleased with himself for his newfound knowledge of dates and places. "But, I know where's he's coming from. I mean I won't be anybody's slave, I gotta be free just like him. It was like he was talking to me when he said, "Is life so dear, or peace so sweet, as to be purchased at the price of chains and slavery? Forbid it, Almighty God! I know not what course others may take, but as for me, give me liberty or give me death!"

In his research Dave discovered all kinds of events that happened before our first Independence Day, July 4, 1776. "Those dudes liked a good fight too," he added, which prompted a discussion about conflict and how it often brings about change in the social order. Another benefit of these monologues is that they offer the chance to discuss issues that come up during the research experience.

Creating historical perspective monologues generates an opportunity to celebrate multiethnic cultural diversity as well. Direct your players to include monologues of famous leaders or personalities from other countries, cultures, and periods in their history. Playing material foreign to one's own identity is one of the most exciting challenges that an actor faces. Viewing history and contemporary events from the perspectives of different ethnic and cultural groups produces new information and understanding for everyone involved.

There are many other sources from which to create historical perspective monologues. Possibilities include biographies, novels, short stories, letters, diaries, autobiographies, newspapers.

## BIOGRAPHICAL NARRATIVE

Your best sources of material are published biographies, letters, or diaries. You can also find newspaper columns from the appropriate period. For example, the author did a biographical narrative of Varina Howell Davis, who was the only first lady of the South, and was married to Jefferson Davis, the president of the Confederate States of America. For that research she discovered back issues on file of the *New York Times* from the 1870s, containing many firsthand accounts of the Civil War and what else was happening in the country on the exact date when various dramatic events occurred in the first lady's life.

Who are some famous people in the twentieth century that your players would like to research for monologues? From the list below of a few of the outstanding individuals of this century, let your participants select one that speaks to them and create a first-person monologue for that character. Once they tune into the reality of the problems that occurred, as well as the conflicts individuals dealt with at the time, they will be able to create more realistic dramatic monologues. Here are some suggestions of people who have made an outstanding contribution to our society in this century. Would some of their lives make interesting material for a monologue?

1. Mother Teresa
2. Martin Luther King, Jr.
3. Jackie Robinson
4. Amelia Earhart
5. Golda Meir
6. Sally Ride
7. Fidel Castro
8. Paul Robeson
9. Michael Jordan
10. Maya Angelou
11. Jonas Salk
12. Jacques Cousteau

Make your own list. Who are your heroes and heroines of today and yesterday? Ask your players to write up their own lists and put all the names together. Pay special attention to the names that appear most frequently. Are there more sports figures than writers and scientists? Direct your participants to select the person they would like to research for a monologue. Urge them to do as much research as necessary to discover what motivated these famous historical figures. What were some personal conflicts they had to resolve in their lives? What were some of the public issues?

## MONOLOGUES WITH PROBLEMS

The next monologue exercise will bring your players back into the present and deal with common problems young people face today. Unlike the research monologue above, this is an improvisational monologue. Once again, you may suggest that your participants write it out first and then read it to the group. Each of your players selects a card with one of the identities below. No doubt you will add ones of your own. Mark the front M or F for male or female roles. It doesn't matter if some players select the same card, because no two people will create the character or play it exactly the same way. Write these character descriptions along with your additional ones on cards. The actor states her name and the problem written on the card. She must add a brief description of the character and her particular personal interpretation of the problem. In role, she will tell us about herself, her past, present, wants, needs, and fears. Encourage the player to create the dramatic conflict any way she chooses. The director may facilitate the monologue by asking questions of the character if she appears stuck. For example a card might read as follows:

> Your name is Diana. You are a 16-year-old girl accused of shoplifting makeup in the local department store. Tell us about yourself. Tell us what happened.

The actor has the choice whether to play the monologue as if he or she is guilty or innocent. The situation for the monologue states only that Diana has been accused. It's up to the player to decide how she wants to act the monologue. One interpretation of the problem above might go something like this:

> Hi, my name is Diana Johnson. I'm sixteen years old, a sophomore in high school, and I don't know what the big deal is. You'd think I stole a diamond ring or something. I said I'd pay for the lousy lipstick, and this clerk thinks it's a federal case. I said a dozen times I'd pay for it but she doesn't listen. Hey, I don't even like the color. "That's not the point," she says. What *is* the point? Now, she's gonna drag in the store detective who's gonna call my mother, who's not home anyway. Even if she were, she wouldn't do anything—probably yell at me and tell me to be more careful next time and not get caught.
>
> It's a big waste of time. They won't do anything to me. I'm under age. They're just trying to scare me. Well, forget it. That doesn't scare me. I'm not afraid of that old lady. I could take her if I wanted to. Why don't they spend their time catching some real crooks or busting drug dealers instead of wasting their time and mine on a lousy lipstick?
>
> (*Raising her voice*) Hey, somebody come back in here. I'm gonna be late for practice. Then I won't make the team. It's all your

fault. I've got rights, you know. You can't keep me here forever. I'm getting sick of this crap. I feel like bustin' up the joint. I just might!

(*She looks at the door indicating another person has entered*) Well, it's about time. Now what? I can go? Why? What's gonna happen now? (*Pause*) She is? My mother's waiting outside. Oh, great! She's gonna be mad havin' to leave work. You'd better just hope she doesn't freak out on you. (*Pause*) Thank you? Thank you for what? Why should I thank you. I told you—I don't even like the color. (*She exits*)

Discuss the feelings of the actor first. What did she feel in the role? At what point did she feel conflict within herself and/or with the other unseen players in her monologue? Ask your participants what they felt watching. What did they learn about the character? Focus on questions that provide insight rather than guilt or innocence. How would someone else play the role? What would you do differently? Maybe this time the actress will play it as if she is falsely accused. Play it again with a different person in the role.

There are more identity cards listed below from which to create other monologues with problems. Prepare your players in the same way as you did for the shoplifting one. You'll notice that several of the identity cards are non–gender specific. These names could be either male or female. Remember, it's up to the individual actor whether he plays the conflict as if he is guilty or innocent.

1. Your name is George. You're seventeen years old and you have been accused of cheating on an exam.
   Tell us about yourself and what happened.
2. Your name is Grace. You're a single mother in her early twenties. You are accused of selling your food stamps. Tell us about yourself and what happened.
3. Your name is Eric and you are in your early twenties. You are accused of abandoning your family. Tell us about yourself and what happened.
4. Your name is Pat. You are a police officer. You are accused of being a racist. Tell us about yourself and what happened.
5. Your name is Kim and you are sixteen. You are accused of smoking pot in the school bathroom. Tell us about yourself and what happened.

6. Your name is Sal and you're seventeen. You are
   accused of stealing a car. Tell us about yourself and what happened.
7. Your name is Mindy. Your best friend accused
   you of trying to steal her boyfriend. Tell us about
   yourself and what happened.
8. Your name is Jonni and you're seventeen. You are accused
   of dealing drugs in school. Tell us about yourself and
   what happened.
9. Your name is Frank. You're sixteen and you're accused
   of driving drunk without a license. Tell us about yourself
   and what happened.
10. Your name is Sharon, age fifteen. You're accused of having a
    drinking party at your house while your parents were away.
    Tell us about yourself and what happened.

Remember to process after each scene. Discuss what the actor felt
in the role. Where was the conflict? Did the actor play it as if he
were guilty or innocent? What prompted his choice? What did the
audience members feel watching? Focus on the feelings of the
player and audience. Phrase your questions in such a way as to
prompt insight and self-examination rather than focus on the guilt
or innocence of the character.

## AUTOBIOGRAPHICAL NARRATIVE

What's the most important subject for all of us? *Me!* That's right.
There's nothing most of us enjoy talking about more than ourselves, even though some may be a bit shy in the beginning. Rather
than recite a litany of dates and places such as "I was born in
Detroit, Michigan, in 1981" (as in the autobiography you probably
wrote in the fourth or fifth grade), this one is different. Some participants may find an autobiographical narrative too demanding
with too much self-disclosure for their comfort.

A good way to put your group members in touch with themselves
is to use the "I am . . ." line. In this exercise you go around the
room as quickly as possible with each player filling in the blank
after the words "I am." You may want to use a metronome or a
drum to keep a rhythm going for their words. It's easier to recognize the pause that eventually occurs that way. To begin, ask for
volunteers and see how many times they can complete the phrase

"I am . . ." without stopping. For example, if the author did this exercise it would look something like this: "I am a professor, wife, mother, writer, therapist, friend, swimmer, reader, listener, correspondent, cleaner, driver, shopper, director, actor, advisor, mentor, student, traveler, cousin, aunt, sister, collector, commuter, typist, dancer. . . . (This is where the pause came.)

If we were playing the game, it would now be the next person's turn to say, "I am a . . ." until he paused, and then the next person would go and so on. One interesting part of this is to consider the order in which the words came out. In the above list the surprise came by how far down the word *director* was. This exercise helps your players realize the many roles they play in life, and gives them a variety of choices from which to begin their autobiographical narratives. As before, you may do this exercise as a written one. Give your participants one minute or so to write down all of their responses to "I am a . . . ," and then ask them to read their lists aloud.

You may want to offer students the option of either creating a fictional character or using their own lives for their autobiographical narratives. This allows participants a margin of safety without the necessity of self-disclosure, but it also keeps them in the playing arena. Another option is to focus on one incident containing a conflict for the monologue. The anecdote can be funny, sad, or inspirational, either fact or fiction. Further, add that players don't have to tell the audience whether their monologue is real or fictional. Part of the fun with this is trying to figure out who spoke about real incidents in their lives and who used their imaginations. Many people embellish or exaggerate their own stories all the time. Of course, it you get a monologue from Xena the warrior princess or Ara the alien from outer space, you'll know it is fiction.

Prime the pump for your players by asking such questions as: "What do you want?" "What is important to you?" "What do you like?" "What do you dislike?" "Think about your past, present, future. Where do you plan to go from here in your life?" "What are some of your life goals?" Whether they make up a story or use their own lives, these questions will give students food for thought. Hopefully, insight will come from what the actor chooses to tell the group about herself and her adventures—real or imagined.

Why not model this monologue with a humorous incident from your own past to begin or if you really want to get participants' imaginations going, invent a tale of some wild escapade from your youth to keep them guessing?

After each monologue, discuss the content and explore the feelings. First, ask the actor how he or she felt during the incident. How was the conflict resolved? Respect all the answers even if some are far out or even bizarre. Young people love to test the limits of authority figures. Then ask your audience, "Has anyone had a similar experience? How did you handle it? What were the conflicts in the experience? Was there anything in the narrative that you particularly identified with? Did it bring back any memories for you?" Remember, you're not trying to find out if the narratives are true or not; you're merely trying to promote some personal examination and insight for the group.


## FUTURE PROJECTION MONOLOGUES

Use a doorway—set piece or a real one—for the first part of this exercise. If that is not possible, simply suggest a magic threshold through which your participants will walk. Direct your players to see themselves as an adult on the other side of the doorway or threshold. The adult is at least ten to fifteen years older than the actor is now. What do they look like? How are they different from the young person they are now? What's their posture? Their attitude? Each participant will describe his or her adult. This can be done all at the same time or you can ask for volunteers. Expect a certain amount of comedy with the initial exercise. The next part is what's really important.

Direct your players to step through the doorway and *become* that adult. Step into the adult's shoes and take on the role of the adult the young person will become. In other words, Bob the high school junior becomes Bob the adult businessman. When Bob has accomplished that to his own satisfaction, direct him to walk back into the scene. The director will place an empty chair in front of Bob the adult. He is to imagine that Bob the young person is seated in the chair. The adult Bob will speak to the empty chair as if the young Bob were seated there.

Begin the monologue with the words, "**You'd better learn how to . . .**" and end with, "**Look where I am now. I am** . . . The young person should fill this last blank with a positive wish for the future.

Instruct your actors to give the young person in the empty chair advice on how to reach the level of success attained by the actor

playing the adult. For example, let's say that Jane (the adult) speaks
to Jane (the young person) in the empty chair. Let the adult Jane
give the young Jane advice on how to reach adulthood successfully.
Jane's monologue could go something like this:

> **You'd better learn how to** . . . say no. You always do everything
> everybody else wants you to do. It's been getting you in trouble
> and you know it. I want you to start saying it right now or you
> won't be me. Go ahead, repeat after me. No. No. No. See how
> easy it is? I make up my own mind about things now. I don't listen
> to what other people want to do. I have my own opinions even if
> I'm wrong sometimes. I make my own mistakes, not because I
> let someone talk me into doing something I didn't want to do. I
> make mistakes, but that's all right, because I don't usually make
> the same one again. I'm not like you anymore. I don't keep doing
> the same stupid things over again.
>
> And another thing, you'd better start standing up for yourself too.
> You can see that I'm not a doormat like you. I don't let anybody
> push me around anymore. I don't want to fight but I don't
> back down. People respect you when you stand up to them.
> There's something else too. I don't like the way you try to get by
> without studying just because you think it's cool.
>
> Oh, yeah, there's one more thing. You'd better learn to chill. You
> take everything too seriously. Everything's always a tragedy with
> you. Lighten up. It's not the end of the world. You know from
> here a lot of your problems look pretty silly. I can't even remem-
> ber half the stuff that bothers you now. See! That's how important
> it is when I look back. I remember the time you cried when you
> thought your hair was cut too short. That was a real tragedy for
> you. Now I'd just laugh and put a hat on.
>
> One last thing, you're not really such a bad kid, you know. You
> just underestimate yourself. Remember what I told you to do.
> That's how you'll get where I am. **Look where I am now** . . . I'm
> married. I have good job and a bank account. And I'm going
> to Mexico on my next vacation. I'm the happy, successful, grown-
> up you!

Beginning male actors sometimes have a harder time with this improvisational monologue. The act of exploring their own feelings aloud in front of others can be threatening for some and downright impossible for others. However, with a little patience and side coaching, you can usually bring them around. You may have to spend more time in the role creation of the adult figure before you begin the monologue. Talk about some of the real role models in the young man's life. What are some of the adult characteristics he hopes to acquire? Does he have a career goal? Suggest that he focus on successfully achieving that goal. Even if it's unrealistic, accept it as the adult role, and help him discover some of the steps necessary to reach that goal. Many teenage boys opt for grandiose celebrity. However, even a basketball star like Michael Jordan had to exercise a lot of self-discipline and put in a lot of practice time before he got where he is. Famous rock stars or rappers also had to put time and effort into their careers. Nobody is suddenly catapulted to lasting fame without putting forth some personal effort.

With this extra coaching and a promise of group support from his peers, a sixteen-year-old named Joe finally acted out his monologue.

> **You'd better learn how to** . . . take things seriously. Everything's a joke with you. Get serious, will you? You'd better if you want to get where I am and have your own landscaping business. You can't be the clown all the time, you know. Like ya gotta start paying attention in class. You're missing too much stuff when you fool around all the time. I know why you do it too and so do you. If you spent as much time studying as you do fooling around, you'd probably get As. You probably could if you wanted to.
>
> I take things seriously now. I still have a good time, but I take my business seriously, and my family. I've got all the good things. Nobody tells me what to do. I do what I want to do. I've been out with lots of girls. Sometimes I just go by myself. I don't have to be with somebody all the time. I like to be outside by myself. Can you handle that?
>
> You'd better start learning. And you better get it together. How you gonna have your own business if you can't do math? Do your math homework, dork. I use math every day. I have to figure out

lots of complicated stuff. How much manure to buy—stuff like that. So you'd better pay attention to that geometry stuff too. You'll need it. So get serious.

**Look where I am now . . .** I've got a business, a car, a house, a fat bank account, a fat wallet, fat kids and—and a skinny wife. (*He laughed and then added*) I couldn't resist the last line.

One junior high school teacher named Ingrid commented, "What I liked about this activity was that it revealed the concerns of the individual students—what they thought needed to change in their lives." She smiled in recall and then continued, "It amazes me how these types of activities excite and bring out so much in the students with behavior problems."

## SUMMARY

Monologues come from a variety of sources and are a well-known theatrical device for exploring the feelings of a character. The monologue can serve beginning players as a way to find their inner voice or the inner voice of the character they are playing. The historical perspective and biographical narrative monologues both require research and exploration to develop a basic understanding of historical events and personalities. Monologues with problem conflicts offer your players an opportunity to use their creative imaginations and character development skills. Autobiographical narratives focus on our favorite subject—me—and can be played as fact or fiction to promote personal examination and insight. Future projection monologues offer actors opportunities to imagine themselves as successful adults who have discovered some of the secrets of success that they can pass on to the youngsters they really are.

# 11

## Short Plays to Act and Complete

There are those who look at things the way they are,
and ask why. . . . I dream of things that never were, and
ask why not?

*Robert Kennedy*

## THEATRE: THE MIRROR OF SOCIETY

Theatre offers us a mirror of our society and of ourselves. Drama can take us out of ourselves, on a journey to another place or state of mind. Drama and theatre give us the opportunity to experience vicariously the pain and pleasure, or the courage and cowardice, of another human being. We have the chance to feel the gamut of human emotions from a safe spot in the audience or even on stage. As any actor knows, when you really get involved in the play, you have all the same emotional reactions you would in the actual life situation. You can laugh, cry, gasp, scream, even have physical reactions such as an accelerated heartbeat, sweaty palms, shortness of breath—all the same physical manifestations you would experience if you were participating in the real action itself. You experience everything *except* the consequences of your actions. You can leave the role on stage and walk away from the theatre as a totally different person from the one you were on stage.

The beauty of this experience is that we can view problems and feel emotions from the safety and anonymity of playing the role or being seated in the audience. Through drama we can probe problems we might feel too uncomfortable to examine in our everyday life. We can listen to conversations that might be embarrassing to overhear in our living room. We can inspect other points of view that might be totally opposed to everything we've been taught. We can become familiar with people and lifestyles very different from our own.

Frequently, you hear famous actors, directors, or writers talk about what prompted them to take their current career paths. They usually say something like "Seeing that play changed my life! I knew I had to work in the theatre," or "That film gave me a new way to look at life, and I had to share that vision with my own film-making," and even "One life is not enough for me. I want to play every role I can."

Theatre offers conflict exploration as an opportunity to discover more about yourself, others, and the world. We need to take a look at conflicts between ideas and realities. The Golden Rule tells us, "Do unto others as you would have them do unto you." But what if the other person has different needs or expectations as in a different culture? What we would have others do for us might not be the same thing he would like done for him. In order to know what his needs or expectations are, we must know something about his culture. Conflicts arise frequently between two people of different cultures who simply see the problem from different perspectives. The difference of opinion in these cases can derive from cultural orientation, but still translate as lack of respect. Let's identify such conflicts, bring them out in the open, and examine them through drama. These are conflicts that the theatre can explore openly and safely.

Schools can provide theatre performances that offer opportunities to become familiar with other races, lifestyles, and cultures to help young people develop *ethnic literacy*. The buzz words these days are *computer literacy*; when are we going to learn *ethnic literacy*, not to mention *emotional literacy*? Are we more concerned with achieving skills at a machine than we are with acquiring life skills? Do we care more about CD-ROMs than about creating understanding among people who are different from each other? Theatre can help build diverse relationships with people. Most of our current classrooms have no process in place for the de-escalation of strong feelings in life situations, but we do have that process available in theatre and the drama. How often do we hear a student say after participating in drama, "I never knew how it was so much fun to play a character different from myself," or "Oh, that felt so good to really get out my anger and not hurt anyone." What people don't realize is that when trouble is left to simmer, it eventually boils over. In other words, one of the advantages of participating in drama/theatre is a good airing out of our emotions.

James A. Banks (1994) points out, "Students are more likely to master important skills when the teacher uses content that deals with significant human problems and issues that relate directly to their life experiences, identification, hopes, dreams and struggles . . . They can achieve skill goals when they study content and problems related to the world in which they live."

The following four short plays, each with a cast of two or three characters, deal with real problems in our society today. You will see the conflicts arise from a challenge to ego, respect, or a reawakening of past grievances, as discussed in Chapter 10.

Victimization becomes a primary issue. What kinds of people and/or situations create victims? Some contributing factors are poverty, drugs, guns, alcoholism, and child abuse. Who are the victims in each of the plays? Is there more than one victim in each piece?

Remember acting the roles in these short plays is only half the process; the discussion afterward, including the examinations of feelings and exploration of alternative solutions, is every bit as important as the play itself. Listen to all contributions and affirm the fact that you are hearing what each participant is offering.

## THE PLAYS

The first play, *The Money*, deals with both ego and past grievances, and centers on drug abuse. The second play, *The Gun*, focuses on past grievances and is a classic victim scenario featuring some of the most common problems: i.e., guns, alcoholism, and child abuse. It offers a clear-cut dramatic structure with a classic conflict. The third play, *The Job*, focuses on respect and deals with bigotry or racism. It adds the element of the instigator, a character outside of the central conflict who urges the perpetrator on to violence. The last play, *The Baby*, explores an age-old problem and focuses on respect.

### THE MONEY

CHARACTERS

Billy, the older brother, 16–17
Sue, the younger sister, 15–16

*The scene is set in the kitchen of an apartment. Billy is standing on a chair struggling to reach something on top of the cabinet, when the door opens and his younger sister Sue enters.*

SUE: What are you doing, Billy?
(*He is shocked by her entrance*)
BILLY (*Gasping*): Jeez, I almost fell. You scared the _____ out of me!
SUE: What are you looking for?
BILLY: None of your business. Aren't you supposed to be in school?
(*He takes something out of jar and puts the jar back on shelf*)
SUE: I threw up. The nurse sent me home. That's mama's money jar. You took the money out of it, didn't you?
(*He climbs down off the stool*)
BILLY: Don't worry about it.
SUE: That's mama's rent money. You'd better put it back.
BILLY: I didn't take nothin'. You're seein' things. Forget it.
SUE: You'd put it back right now or I'm calling mama.
BILLY: Don't be a snitch. She won't need it until the first of the month. It's not even all there yet. I'll put it back by then. I need another ten dollars. Can you give me a loan?
(*He stuffs the money in his pocket*)
SUE: You're using again, aren't you? You promised you'd stop.
BILLY: I will . . . I will . . . just as soon as I get things straightened out.
SUE: That's what you always say. I'm calling mom.
(*She goes to the phone. He grabs her arm to stop her.*)
BILLY: I told you I'd put it back. Now—chill! (*Turning on his charm*) I need another ten dollars, Sweet Sue. I know you've got it from baby-sitting last night.
SUE: Well, you're not getting it. (*Rubbing her arm*) You hurt me. I'm calling mom.
BILLY (*Grabbing her hard*): Don't make me hurt you again. You're not calling anybody. Just forget it. Come on, just a measly ten dollars.
SUE: No! Let go of me. Let go of me or I'll scream.
BILLY: (*Twisting*) You do and I'll break your arm. (*Lightens up and turns on the charm*) You know I'm only kidding. I wouldn't hurt you, Sweet Sue.
SUE (*In pain*): Well, let go. I won't scream.

BILLY: (*Still holding on to her*) And no phone calls either. Don't try to be cute now, Suzie-Q.

SUE (*Reluctantly*): All right. No phone calls. (*He lets go*) Why, Billy? Why are you still shooting that stuff?

BILLY: Because it makes me feel good. All right! You ought to try it sometime. Then maybe you'd understand. Come on, where's your ten?

SUE (*Instinctively reaches for her pocket, then stops realizing she has given herself away.*): You used to say you felt good when you ran track.

BILLY: Shut up. I don't want to hear it. Come on, it's in your pocket. Give it to me. I gotta go meet somebody. You can come with me?

SUE: No! I'm staying here. I have a stomachache, remember?

BILLY: All right, just give me the ten, Sweet Sue. I gotta meet the man, and he don't give discounts. (*His irritation rising*) Come on. I'm hurting'.

SUE (*Sitting on chair*): No, I'm not going to contribute for you to shoot that stuff in your arm.

BILLY: (*Turning on his charm again*) Come on, I know you got it right in your pocket. Don't make me take it away from you. You might get hurt.

> (*She jumps up and tries to run past him into the bathroom. He runs after her but she manages to slip free and goes into the bathroom and locks the door. He is frustrated but stays cool.*)

Come on, Suzie-Q. I'll pay you back. It's only a lousy ten dollars. (*Pauses*) All right stay there. Stay there all day, see if I care.

> (*He pulls the phone jack out*)

The phones not working. I took out the chord.

> (*He bangs on the bathroom door.*)

I can smash it in and your face too. (*Changes his tone of voice*) I was only kidding. You know I wouldn't hurt you. Come on out, Sis. You don't have to go with me, just give me the ten dollars. Push it under the door and don't come out till I leave.

> (*He waits but there's no answer*)

All right, have it your way!

> (*He walks to the outside door and slams it. Walks back silently to the bathroom door and stands waiting for her to come out.*)

**BLACKOUT**

Discuss what feelings the play triggered in the actors first. Then ask questions of the audience. Was there an emotional reaction felt by the audience members? What did they see happen at the end of the play? Talk about that. How did it end? Although Sue is clearly the victim in this play, Billy is his own victim as well. Is he the only source of conflict Sue is dealing with, or is she also in conflict with herself? Does she mind being called a snitch? Ask the actress who played Sue what she felt in the role. What do you think it's like trying to talk to someone who is using dope? How about Billy? What did he feel in the role he played? How was the conflict resolved? What do you think happened when the bathroom door opened? Ask your audience what they felt watching and then discuss how the conflict could be resolved. The obvious resolution, of course, would be that when Sue opened the door, he grabbed her and took the money. Within the given circumstances of the script, what were Sue's options for resolving the conflict? A few possible choices include

1. She could have walked out when she realized that Billie was using again.
2. She could have screamed for help.
3. She could have given Billy the additional ten dollars.
4. She could have stayed in the bathroom, and waited him out.
5. She could have flushed the ten dollars down the toilet.

Can you think of any others? Brainstorm with your players to see what other ways they can think of to resolve this conflict. Others that came up in a tenth-grade classroom were "She could crawl outside from the bathroom window," and "Sue could scream out the bathroom window for help." Focus on Sue's behavior as the one who can change, since she is the problem solver in this play. Listen to all suggestions and examine each possibility offered.

It would be interesting to replay the script using a female Billie and change the Sue role to Sam. You might want to make Sam a little younger so that the physical action will remain believable. Decide if your players want to act the script as written or improvise another method of resolving the conflict.

## THE GUN

## CHARACTERS

The mother
The daughter  Rose
The male voice   (Unseen only heard)

*The scene opens in a bedroom. The mother is sewing up the hem on the daughter's dress.*

MOTHER: It's gonna look so pretty on you, Rosie. I bet you'll be the prettiest girl there.

ROSE: Oh, ma, there's lots of girls prettier than I am.

MOTHER: Not to me. Hand me my sewing box.

(*Rose picks up box and examines the weight*)

ROSE: What have you got in there, a brick? It's so heavy.

MOTHER: Never mind. Just give it to me.

(*Rose hands it to her mother. Rose and Mother are startled by a loud door bang from the next room, and we hear some loud male swearing. Sounds of stumbling and more muttering.*)

MALE VOICE: (*His voice is always heard coming from another room*) Where are my girls? I'm home . . . I wanna see my girls. (*He slurs his words as if drunk*)

MOTHER (*Loudly*): I'll be right there.

(*She helps Rose out of dress and puts sewing things away*)

ROSE: Mama, why did you marry him?

MOTHER: He used to be different.

ROSE: I don't remember him being any different.

MOTHER: I thought he was.

(*There is a loud crash*)

ROSE: He hurts you sometimes, doesn't he?

MOTHER: He doesn't mean to. It's only when he drinks.

MALE VOICE: Hey, where's the beer?

ROSE (*Frightened*): He sounds like he's drunk again, Ma. Don't let him hurt you.

(*She puts on a robe*)

MOTHER: I'll get him something to eat quick. He'll be all right.

MALE VOICE: Where's my dinner? A man wants dinner on the table when he gets home from work.

(*Bangs on table*)

ROSE (*Sarcastically*): Since when does he work till nine o'clock?

MOTHER: Shh! (*She goes to door and opens it*) You're late. I'll have to warm something up for you.

MALE VOICE: I don't want leftovers, I want dinner, woman. (*Coming closer and shouting*) Now get out here before I come in and drag you out. (*More loud noises as if he has knocked something over and muttered curses.*)

ROSE: (*Grabbing her mother's arm*) I'm afraid, Mama. That's how he was the last time when he was pointing that gun at us.

MOTHER (*Reassuring her*): Don't worry about that gun. I put it someplace where he'd never look.

ROSE: Shall I call uncle Lou to come down from upstairs? I can go out the fire escape.

MALE VOICE: God, woman, there's not even any beer in the refrigerator. What good are you?
(*Another crash*) Get out here.

MOTHER: No, don't call Lou. I can handle him. You stay in here, Rosie, and lock the door. Don't come out, do you hear me? Don't come out.
(*She exits from bedroom door*)

ROSE: I could call the police from the corner.

MOTHER (*From the hall*): Lock the door, Rosie.
(*Rose locks the door and leans against it fearfully. Shouts of anger, and sounds of a knock-down-drag-out fight. There is a painful scream from within and Rose opens the door and looks out.*)

ROSE (*She stays in the door way*): Stop it! Stop it or I'll call the police!

MALE VOICE: You little bitch, shut your mouth or you'll get the same.

MOTHER (*Through muffled sobs*): Rosie, get inside. Lock the door.
(*Rose does so and leans against the door in fear and panic. She hears another loud scream and the sound of something falling then a rising scream, "Nooooooo!" Rose is frantic and then she repeats what her mother said about the gun.*)

ROSE: Where he'd never look. (*She quickly looks around the room. Then she sees the sewing basket on the bed.*) I'll bet . . .
(*She takes out a gun and fiddles with it for a moment releasing the safety catch. She moves quickly to the door and opens it. Stands in the doorway with the gun in her hand.*)

ROSE (*Shouting*): Stop it, don't you hit her again.

MALE VOICE (*Laughing*): You gonna tell me what to do? You stupid little bitch.

MOTHER'S VOICE: No, Rosie, no!

MALE VOICE: You want to hurt me, do you? Gimme that thing, and I'll show you who's going to get hurt.

*(She steps out of the doorway into the hall. The bedroom is now empty. Sound of a gunshot, then silence as the lights slowly fade)*

**BLACKOUT**

The violence and the male perpetrator are purposely kept offstage, so that the imagination can supply the character and the action. Discuss what feelings the play triggered in the actors first. Then ask questions of the audience. What did they feel watching the play? Was there an emotional reaction felt by the audience members? What did they see happen at the end of the play? Talk about that. Did Rose shoot the man? Who was the victim in this play? Actually, all three characters are victims. The mother was a victim. If the man was shot, he was a victim. If Rose shot the man, she is a victim of her own anger.

Discuss how else this conflict could have been resolved. What were Rose's other options offered in the play?

1. Go upstairs and bring down her Uncle Lou
2. Go to the corner and call the police
3. Stay in the room and do nothing
4. Confront the man without taking the gun

Was there anything else she could do to resolve the conflict without resorting to this kind of violence? Talk about other possible ways to deal with the conflict. Remember, Rose's behavior is the only one that can change in this scenario.

Decide if your participants want to replay the script and allow Rose to improvise a different ending. Perhaps they can come up with a conclusion that wasn't suggested in the play. Once again, listen to all suggestions and examine the possibilities.

## THE JOB

### CHARACTERS

Mr. Johnson   The manager
Joe   A worker
Larry   Another worker

*Mr. Johnson, the boss, and Larry, a worker, are of the same race or ethnic background, either black, white, or Hispanic. Joe is of a different color or ethnic background. If you decide to use a Hispanic player or want to change the names, feel free to do so.*

*The scene is set in a fast food restaurant before opening. Larry is busy preparing for the day's business as Joe enters.*

LARRY (*Surprised*): Hey, it's your day off. What are you doing here?

JOE: Where's Mr. Johnson? I thought he said he'd tell us today about his decision.

LARRY: What decision? What are you talking about? He's not gonna like you hangin' around if you're not working.

JOE: Which one of us is going to be his assistant manager.

LARRY (*Laughing*): You don't really think there's any question, do you?

JOE: What do you mean?

LARRY: You're wasting your time. That man takes care of his own. Go home.

JOE: He said he was going to check time cards, days off, who was late, and who got customer evaluations . . . all that stuff.

LARRY: Grow up, kid. Do you see anybody like you moving up in this place?

JOE: You know I work harder than you do . . . put in more hours. You're goofin' off half the time.

LARRY: So what! You think any of that matters to Johnson? He thinks all you people are the same.

JOE: You mean he's prejudiced? [a racist, a bigot, choose the word]

LARRY: You said it, I didn't. What do you think?

(*Mr. Johnson enters*)

MR. JOHNSON: Get busy, you lazy bums, we open in fifteen minutes.

LARRY (*Salutes and snapping to*): Yes, sir. Joey ain't even working today. He's just hanging around.

JOE: It's my day off, Mr. Johnson. I just came in to see if you made up your mind yet?

MR. JOHNSON: Make up my mind? What are you blabbering about? If you're not working, get out of the way. You know I don't like kids in here when they're not working.

JOE: You said yesterday you'd tell us today who's gonna be the new assistant manager.

MR. JOHNSON (*Looking hard at him like he's some creature from outer space*): There were people in here. I had to say that. Grow up, kid.

JOE: What do you mean?

MR. JOHNSON: What is it with you people, are you all stupid too?

JOE (*Getting angry*): Don't talk to me like that!

MR. JOHNSON (*Confrontational*): I'll talk to you any damn way I please. I'm the boss here. Now get the hell out.

JOE: I just asked a question.

MR. JOHNSON (*Winking at Larry who laughs and eggs him on*): So you are stupid. What do you say we call him Stupid from now on, Larry? What do you think?

LARRY: Sure, Mr. Johnson, "stupid" suits him just fine.

JOE: I don't have to take this from anybody. (*Angry*)

MR. JOHNSON: You don't like it, you know what you can do. There's the door.

JOE: Did you ever hear of affirmative action?

MR. JOHNSON: You threatening me, kid? Yeah! I heard of affirmative action. You want to see affirmative action? I'll show you some *real* affirmative action.

(*He steps toward Joe aggressively*)

LARRY (*Egging him on to fight*): Show him, boss. He thinks he's better than us.

(*Grabbing a knife from the counter*)

JOE: Look, I don't want to fight, but . . .

MR. JOHNSON (*Laughing*): Ha! That's a mistake, kid.

LARRY: Get 'em, Mr. Johnson get the _____ [insert word]

MR. JOHNSON (*Menacing*): Watch this, Larry. We're gonna teach this boy a lesson he'll never forget!

JOE (*Puts down knife*): I don't want to fight you.

MR. JOHNSON: Too late, _____ [insert word, i.e.,white boy, black boy, spic]! You're gonna show some respect!

(*He starts toward him*)

LARRY: Get 'em! Get 'em!

**BLACKOUT**


Once again, ask the actors to examine their feelings in the roles they played and share what they felt with the audience. Pay particular attention to the feelings erupting from the conflicts that exploded into anger. After you have explored those feelings, ask the audience members the same questions. What did they feel watching the play? What did they see happen after the blackout? Did Mr. Johnson beat up Joe or could there be more than one possible ending? The victim in this piece was clear-cut. Don't be surprised if audience members felt or saw something different from what the players felt. Sometimes audience members even see things differently while watching the same performance. This illustrates an important point of how different perceptions can derive from the same set of given circumstances. In other words, two people can watch the same highly charged conflict, and see it in different ways. Discuss how else the conflict could have been resolved. What were Joe's options other than the fight offered in the play? Those mentioned in the script were

1. He could leave right away when Larry told him the boss didn't like employees in the place on their day off.
2. He could leave when Mr. Johnson said "You know I don't like kids in here when they're not working," or "Get the hell out," or "There's the door."
3. He could say something like "I see my timing is really bad. I'll save it for another time."
4. Don't mention affirmative action to him.
5. Ask to speak to Mr. Johnson in private.

Was there anything else he could do to resolve the conflict without resorting to violence? Remember that Joe's behavior is the only one that can change in this scenario. Listen to all suggestions and examine the possibilities. Talk about the role that Larry played in the drama. How did he escalate the confrontation?

Here's a good place to talk about affirmative action and what it is, if you choose to. Would Joe have been better off not to mention it to Mr. Johnson and simply file an affirmative action suit stating racial or ethnic bias in being refused the promotion?

Replay the script with the opposite ethnic character types and see how differently it plays. Use any of the suggested alternatives or play it again as scripted before you try the alternatives. How was it different? You may want to do it several ways. Was anyone able to resolve the conflict before it burst into full-blown anger? Remember to listen to all suggestions and discuss possible alternatives.

## THE BABY

### CHARACTERS

Sheri  A young girl of about fifteen or sixteen
Bob    A young boy about the same age

*The scene is set in a park near school. SHERI and BOB are seated with a wide space between them on the park bench.*

BOB: Boy, that's some bombshell to drop on a guy. Are you sure?
SHERI: I'm sure.
BOB: Did you take the test?
SHERI: I took the test.
BOB: Maybe it was a mistake. Try it again.
SHERI: There was no mistake.
BOB: Well, what do you want me to do about it?
SHERI: I don't know. I thought we could figure that out together.
BOB: How do I know it's even mine? You got around a lot before we started.
SHERI: You know you were the first. You told me nothing could happen the first time . . . remember?
BOB: So maybe you lied and it wasn't your first time.
SHERI: Bob, stop it! You told me you loved me.
BOB: I did—*then.*
SHERI: What's that supposed to mean? That you don't love me now?
BOB: I don't know. (*Nervously*) I just didn't expect this to happen.
SHERI: Well, I didn't expect it either. You're the one who said you didn't need—
BOB: Oh, so it's all my fault, is that it?
SHERI: No, I didn't say that, but you said it couldn't happen.
BOB: Well, girls can take care of that kind of stuff. You should've done something.
SHERI: Like what?
BOB (*Half-jokingly*): Well, you could always fall down a flight of stairs or something.
SHERI (*Angry*): Or maybe somebody could push me!
BOB: Look, I don't care what you do, just leave me out of it.
SHERI: It's too late for that. You're already in it.
BOB: You're the one who screwed up.

SHERI (*Hurt*): Now it's my fault?

BOB: Does your mother know?

SHERI: Are you kidding? My mom would kill me—

BOB: Now, there's a solution!

SHERI: And you!

BOB: I don't like that part. (*Sarcastically*) I'm too young to die.

SHERI: Shut up. It's not funny.

BOB: Oh, thanks for telling me.

SHERI (*Demanding*): What are we going to do?

BOB: I don't know what to do. (*Grasping at straws*) Take one of those morning-after pills or something.

SHERI: It's too late for that.

BOB: Well, do something! It's your problem. *You* solve it.

(*He starts to leave*)

I gotta go before I lose it.

SHERI: Wait. You want me to solve it. All right, I've got a great idea. See how you like this.

(*She starts after him as he exits*)

(*Yelling sarcastically after him*) I could always kill myself! Would that make you happy?

(*She returns to the bench and sits*)

Yeah, I could kill myself.

(*Sighs*) Or you!

**BLACKOUT**

Even though the primary conflict in this play is between Sheri and Bob, each one of them has an inner conflict as well. Is Sheri the only victim or are both Bob and Sheri victims? Ask your players to examine the feelings each had in playing their roles and share them with the audience. How did members of the audience feel watching this piece? What feelings were triggered for them? Discuss their feelings as well.

What were the solutions to resolve this conflict offered in the play? Were any of them acceptable?

1. Take the test again
2. Fall or pushed down the stairs
3. "My mother would kill me."
4. Kill myself or you

Was this conflict resolved? What suggestions can the audience come up with? There are three obvious options that didn't come out specifically in the script: abortion, marriage and/or raising the baby themselves, having the baby and offering him or her up for adoption. It will be interesting to note which of these alternatives comes up first in your brainstorming with the audience. Listen to all suggestions and examine each of the possibilities.

Once again replay the script using any of the solutions suggested by your audience. This might be an interesting script in which to use POV-doubles for each of the characters. You can also use this as a playwriting activity. A high school English teacher suggested, "Divide your players into separate teams. After they have acted out their solution, ask them to write or script their resolution scene. Remind them that the POV character is the one that has to solve the problem. Ask them to read that scene aloud after it's complete."

## SUMMARY

Conflict is essential to all drama. The theatre offers us the emotional experience of others in actual life situations within the safety of playing a role or as a member of the audience. Through drama we can probe problems we might feel too uncomfortable to examine in everyday life. We can become familiar with people and lifestyles different from our own. Theatre can help build diverse relationships with people. Participating in drama offers us exercise for the imagination and intellect, as well as a good airing out of our emotions. Remember, acting the roles in the short plays above is only half the process. The discussion afterward, including the examination of feelings and the exploration of alternative solutions, is as important as the play itself. The significant thing about practicing additional possibilities in conflict resolution is that it gets people into the habit of looking for alternatives in the situation rather than settling for the first answer that pops into their heads.

# 12

# Create Your Own
# Play or Video

The structure of a play is always the story of how the
birds came home to roost."

*Arthur Miller*

All plays begin with a story whether they are written for stage, film,
or video. The story is what matters, and what propels the story forward is conflict. The play requires a strong, clear-cut conflict with
obstacles blocking the goal. The structure of a play and the structure of a screenplay are similar in having a beginning, a middle,
and an end. George M. Cohan, the famous actor and composer,
put it this way:

Get 'em up a tree
Throw stones at 'em
Get 'em down.

Put another way, the play has a problem, complication, and solution (or resolution). Syd Field, the famous screenwriting teacher
says, "All drama is conflict. Without conflict you have no character,
without character, you have no action, without action, you have no
story, and without story, you have no screenplay" (Field 1994, 21).
    There are three components to any script: plot, character, and
dialogue. Screenwriters add a fourth component—setting. Scripts
for plays have different formats from those used for movies and
videos, as will be illustrated later in this chapter. Many excellent
books are available on playwriting, screenwriting, and writing for

TV, a selection of which are listed in the bibliography. For our purposes in this chapter, only a simplified overview of dramatic structure will be discussed.

Playwriting requires insight into human nature, an understanding of what makes people tick, as well as an understanding of cause and effect. It takes the ability to verbalize thoughts and feelings. It is supreme in the written genres for the mastery of language skills. Yet it is one of the most accessible literary forms because it begins with the spoken word. We read words to ourselves and sometimes read aloud. Words are part of our daily lives; we produce them every day and hear others use them. Words exhibit a life of their own in our imaginations. For example, you might catch yourself thinking, "When I say it's not my fault then he'll say _____ and I'll tell him I'm sorry and he'll say _____ ." Words are with us most of our waking hours and often in our dreams as well.

Playwriting offers your participants exercise for the imagination, emotional reactions to conflict situations, and insight into other people's feelings. It teaches more than conflict resolution alone. As the facilitator you're teaching your young playwrights a variety of additional skills as well, e.g., listening, critical thinking, logic, cooperation, interpersonal communication, and creative writing.

The Young Playwrights program sponsored by the Foundation of the Dramatists Guild says in their brochure entitled "Good Teachrs Teach—Great Teachers LEARN," "We believe that all students can write plays and that all teachers can teach playwriting." Creating a play with others is a perfect example of cooperative learning. It teaches your players to listen to others and to accept their ideas, to weigh and balance all choices offered, and to put the needs of the play before personal needs for recognition. The project's success will depend on the players' ability to work cooperatively and to accept and understand each other.

Writing a play is hard work. It's also an exciting and mind-expanding adventure. Some participants find it hard to recognize that other people have a point of view different from theirs. Not everyone sees the world in the same way. Theatre offers the players, as well as the audience, a chance to see the world through someone else's eyes. It feeds the imagination with a range of experiences much broader than those most youngsters have in their personal lives or what they see on television. It's important to select and discuss examples of conflicts that are resolved effectively and those that are not. What are the differences? What are the causes? It's important to recognize which obstacles were set up that prevented the resolution of the conflict.

Collaboration is never easy, but it works best when there is mutual respect among the participants. Ideally, you would want your groups to be made up of equally creative talents. Most professional collaborators are made up of two or three on a team, and each member of the team has similar talents but different special strengths in one or more areas. An example of this kind of collaboration is found in Broadway musicals. One person writes the book, another the lyrics, and yet another composes the music. That's a three-way collaboration. Sometimes more than one person writes the book, several work on the lyrics, and others contribute as well. The same is true for screenwriting. At times six or seven writers are listed on a film.

An interesting trend on Broadway today is what is called *the workshop production*. This means that the play or musical was created by a series of improvisational workshops, and a variety of performers contributed to the production. Sometimes the production goes through a series of many workshops, with a number of performers, directors, and contributors to the book. In other words, the professional theatre has discovered the value of group collaboration. Two recent examples of phenomenally successful shows that were created in that way are *A Chorus Line* and *Rent.*

## GETTING STARTED

Selecting the story idea comes first. You may want to assign your players a story they already know for dramatization as their first playwriting exercise. If they begin their plays with an existing story or one you are currently using in your curriculum, they will already have their plot and characters, and sometimes part of the dialogue. It's easier to begin that way. That can be a good first go-round with the collaborative playwriting experience. Divide your players into groups of four to six, no more. Ask them to select a short story from the literature in the curriculum or take a story from history or current events.

Pick a short story that you know well and ask all the groups to work on the same one. Let's use *The Cask of Amontillado* by Edgar Allan Poe as an example. This story can be found in most collections of Poe's works as well as classic short story collections. It is a tale of revenge with only two characters. The teller of the tale,

Montresor, appeals to Fortunato's vanity regarding his ability as a wine connoisseur and lures him to his underground wine vaults ostensibly to test the authenticity of a wine, the Cask of Amontillado. In reality he plans to punish Fortunato for his past insults by walling him up in the vault. It is a good story to dramatize because it has a simple conflict—problem, complications, and solution— and the story itself includes so much dialogue. As a play it would have two locations; as a film it could show a great many more pictures of the vaults as the pair moved from one to the next. However, in the last scene with Fortunato inside the vault, it would be the filmmaker's choice from whose point of view to shoot the scene. The camera could focus on Fortunato chained to the wall as he saw the bricks going into place or from the outside watching Montresor, the teller of the tale, put each brick into place and seal up the wall. Direct your players to read the dialogue between the two men in the first scene where Montresor seduces Fortunato by appealing to his vanity to volunteer to come to his wine cellar to test the Amontillado wine. That scene would end when Fortunato insists on going to the vaults with Montresor with his line, "Let us go, nevertheless. The cold is merely nothing. Amontillado! You have been imposed upon. And as for Luchesi, he cannot distinguish sherry from Amontillado."

On this note the two characters hurry to the palazzo of Montresor, so that Fortunato can prove his expertise. The trap is set.

The climax or high point of action occurs in the next section of the story; inside the vault when Montresor chains Fortunato to the wall. The problem is further complicated when Fortunato tries to laugh off his imprisonment as a joke. He realizes only too late what has happened when he cries out, "For the love of God, Montresor!"

The solution or resolve, of course, is the vengeance that Montresor takes on his victim, and he leaves him with the Latin words *In pace requiescat!* (Rest in peace.)

Direct your players to improvise each of the three sections of the story one at a time. After they have played the story as written, they may want to add some of their own ideas to it by answering some of the questions posed by the story, such as "What did Fortunato do to Montresor to cause a need for such revenge?"

This exercise will whet the appetites of your group for more work and creating their own plays. The playwriting goal is to facilitate writing something based on history, current events, or personal life situations. This calls for new concepts and terms, and also requires your players to reason at a high level and to think critically about the information given. Most participants are eager to explore the more engaging issues involved in their own lives to create material to dramatize.

## FINDING ISSUES AND THEMES

Before you get started on finding your themes to dramatize, remind your players not to imitate their favorite television shows or action film thriller. This is to be their own script, not a warmed-over version of something they've already seen. Encourage them to use themes or issues that they are familiar with in their own lives. Issue-oriented plays that deal with some familiar problems stimulate more passion and excitement among the participants when they are challenged to write original work. Creating characters necessitates understanding what makes people alike and what makes them different. Diversity is necessary in creating characters, and accepting that diversity in drama is inevitable and carries over into human life. What characterization teaches us is that "different" doesn't mean inferior or superior. Differences in dramatic characters are as natural as differences in people.

Good playwrights are good observers, and all observation and memory is sensory. Writers offer us *sense memories* all the time. We've all had the sensation of walking in a strange place and smelling something that immediately took us back to another time and place. That delectable aroma may transport you back to your grandmother's kitchen or a special garden in the summer. At any rate, all of our sense memories are linked to one or more of the five senses; sight, sound, touch, smell, and taste.

Whether you choose to work from a known story or jump right in with your players creating their own story, begin by dividing your participants into groups of four to six. You, as the director of this project, may want to give this selection some careful thought beforehand. Ideally, you want each of the groups to have a balance of strengths, with good skills in imagination, critical thinking, and creative writing. You'll also want to include someone with good verbal skills, and someone who can keep the ball rolling, a team coordinator who gets along well with the others. Those players would make up your playwriting team. You may have to add another member and/or settle for less than the perfect collaboration, but do try for a balance of skills in each group.

Once you have your teams in place, bounce around some possible issues, themes, and/or ideas for the plays. Common problems in society deal with poverty, drugs, alcoholism, and child abuse. Victimization issues fill the headlines today, including random street crime, domestic violence, racial-bias-related violence, dating abuse, child abuse. Encourage your players to look at the role of conflict in their own lives. Try asking some of the questions below to promote discussion. Encourage your participants to express a range of responses concerning violence and victimization. Some questions to prime the pump include the following:

1. What is the effect of violence on individuals? On families? On communities? On society?
2. What are some of the issues related to victimization? Why is there victimization by and among young people?
3. Where is violence learned? (friends, family, TV, films?)
4. What are some of society's mixed messages about violence? (Mike Tyson biting his opponent and being paid thirty million dollars for the fight?)
5. Where do you see violence in life? (sports, community, school, home?)
6. What are the emotions we feel associated with violence? (fear, anger, excitement?)
7. What are our choices in dealing with violence? (fight, flight, communicate)
8. What are some examples of nonviolent abuse? (verbal abuse, put-downs, name-calling, diminishing self-esteem)
9. What are some of the contributors to violence? (frustration, boredom, own victimization)
10. What actions can young people take to prevent violence?

As the director of the discussion, elicit as many ideas as possible. Help to define the problems as they are offered. Ask questions that will provoke critical thinking. Probe for more information on general issues. Stay away from personal questions or promoting self-revelation. Keep your discussion in the safety of being focused on the play. If the discussion becomes too personal, acknowledge the contribution but return the discussion to the format of plot, character, and dialogue, for example, "That would make a good conflict incident for your play," or "Your resolution to that incident would be an excellent line of dialogue for the character in your play." During your discussion, maintain the safe, nonjudgmental environment of the dramatist in search of material for play building.

Remind your group that the play is a story with a main problem. (It can have several smaller ones.) There are obstacles or complications in solving that problem. Finally, there is a resolution or solution to the problem.

Who are the characters in the play? Let's say one group decides to start with a new student in a high school named Joe, who wants to stay out of trouble. His would-be girlfriend, Linda, knows how things are run at this school and expects Joe to fit in. The problem character is Flip, the gang leader, who runs the show here at Somewhere High and expects others to follow suit and do things his way. He is feared and respected by the other students. Fill out the rest of the characters as you go. Most players like to get to the action as soon as possible in their playwriting.

Suggest that your participants start with the *"what if..."* technique.

What if there was a young man in love with a young woman . . .
What if their families were sworn enemies . . .
What if the young people defied their parents and married . . .

And so on as Romeo and Juliet head toward the final tragedy. But that's the idea. The "what if . . ." technique is a simple brainstorming of the imagination. Ask one of your groups to illustrate the technique for the others with the following example:

There is a gang in control of a school and neighborhood, but a newcomer named Joe doesn't want to join the gang. What if . . .

the gang threatened to beat him up if he didn't
his older brother was killed in a gang fight
he promised his mother when his brother died he'd never join a gang
his girlfriend Linda thinks he's a coward
he sets up a meeting with the gang
he fights and gets beaten up

How does he solve the problem or resolve it? What other obstacles does he have to overcome? How does his character affect his actions? What is his conflict style? What is the conflict style of the others in the play? Who uses fight, flight, or communicate? How does the conflict style influence the plot?

After the group has come up with several "what if . . ." instances, direct them to act out improvisations based on each important scene that they came up with. For example, the first scene to improvise in the above outline might be when the gang leader and a couple members of the gang meet Joe and invite him to join the gang. He turns them down and is threatened with violence unless he changes his mind.

The second improvisation could be between Joe and his new girlfriend. She might begin by congratulating him on being asked to join the most important gang at the school. When he tells her he has turned them down, she doesn't understand and accuses him of being a coward.

You get the idea. Direct your players to come up with their main story idea or problem, which is the plot. List the characters in the play, and then brainstorm using the "what if . . ." technique. Give students plenty of time to come up with their play idea or theme, to create the characters, and to discuss various conflicts they might use before they resolve the problem. The improvising section will offer some new insight into the problems and characters.

Once participants have their story line pretty well worked out (and this won't happen fast—it takes time), select one person in the group to be the scribe. The scribe will write down the action of each scene, or the players can take turns as the scribe. Before they begin writing the actual script, instruct the group to collaborate on outlining the central and minor conflicts in the play based on the action they decided upon for each scene. Together they will rough out the story line for the scribe to write down. The collaborators decide what incidents they will include in the play.

Now comes the hard work for the players. Encourage each member's cooperation in scripting one of the scenes in the play. Remind them that playwriting is sharing and collaborating. It's hard to recognize that other people have a different point of view from yours. Most of us expect everyone to perceive the world as we do. One thing is certain, your participants will learn a new appreciation for drama and the playwright.

As mentioned earlier, a stage play uses a different format from that used for a screenplay or video. The basic difference is that a screenplay or video is a story told *visually* with pictures and action,

action, action. You can have dozens of scenes and as many characters, with no limits on the environments in which the action takes place. You can use close-ups to show a tear in the corner of the character's eye or you can pan in on the ring on her finger. The play, on the other hand, is a story told in *dialogue*. Characters and what they say are the important elements here. Everything has to be bigger on the stage than it does in a film. However, the sets are limited, as are the number of characters in the play. The play format was illustrated in the last chapter, but it is reviewed below.

## PLAY FORMAT

### JOE'S DECISION
by
Patricia Sternberg

*The scene opens on a bench in front of a high school. Students pass by carrying books. Flip leans on the bench with one foot on the seat. He is chewing on a tooth pick and displays an attitude of boredom. Blinky and Bo are draped casually on the bench. Sound of school bell.*

BLINKY: Here he comes. I told you he'd come.

BO (*Jumping in quickly*): Sure he's comin'. Why wouldn't he?

FLIP (*His manner and attitude tell us he's the leader of this group*):
Shut up. I wanta talk to him.
(*Joe enters and looks around. Sees Flip and heads toward him*)
Yo, Joe. Let's talk.
(*Joe crosses to him*)

JOE: What about?

FLIP (*Not moving from his position*): Your future.

BO: Yeah, about your future.

FLIP (*To Bo, sharply*): Shut up, retard. I'm talkin' to the man.
(*Bo backs up behind the bench*)
(*Changing his tone*) We been lookin' you over, kid.

JOE: Yeah . . . so?

FLIP: We might find a place for you with the Ravens.

BLINKY: Yeah, man, you're lucky. Flip thinks you got what it takes.

FLIP: (*Giving Blinky a light shove for effect, taking back control*) Will you shut up while I'm talkin'? (*To Joe*) No manners, these guys got no manners. (*He eyes Joe curiously*) There's an initiation, of course. What do you say?

(SOUND of SCHOOL BELL)

JOE: There's the bell. I don't want to be late for math.

BLINKY: (*stepping forward and getting in Joe's face*) Answer the man.

BO (*Stepping forward*): Yeah, answer the man.

JOE (*Looking directly at Flip*): I—I eh . . . I want to think about it.

FLIP (*Casually*) : What's to think about? Either you're with us or you're against us. You'd better make up your mind. . . . (*Menacingly*) now!

> (*Linda enters, runs in and grabs Joe's hand, but FLIP steps in front of him and confronts her*)

LINDA: Come on, Joe, you promised me your math homework. (*To Flip turning on the charm*) Give me a break, Flip.

> (*Flip steps aside, and Linda and Joe exit*)

FLIP (*He stands looking after them and punches his fist in his hand*) No manners. That kid's got no manners. I'm gonna have to see he gets some lessons.

(*Bo and Blinky nod approvingly*)

(SOUND OF SCHOOL BELL)

**BLACKOUT**

Now let's take a look at the same scene as it would be written for the screen or TV. This screenplay format will show only the basic differences and won't go into specific camera directions, angles, lighting, and so on. One obvious difference is that the dialogue takes prominence in a play and the directions take prominence in a screenplay or TV script. In a screenplay this scene would be the set-up scene, which defines the tone and the location of the action. This is not a shooting script but merely illustrates the format to serve as a guide for your players. If they decide to video their script, refer to one of the texts listed in the bibliography for a sample of a shooting script.

## SCREENPLAY FORMAT

### JOE'S DECISION

FADE IN

EXTERIOR: PARK BENCH IN FRONT OF HIGH SCHOOL

We see THREE YOUNG MEN longing on the bench with one obviously in the authority position

SOUND OF A SCHOOL BELL

BLINKY steps forward and points.

> BLINKY
> Here he comes. I told you he'd come.
> (He has a satisfied smirk on his face.)

> BO
> (Jumping in quickly)
> Sure he's comin'. Why wouldn't he?

(FLIP looks up. His manner and attitude tell us he's the leader of the group)

> FLIP
> Shut up. I wanna talk to him.
> (LONG SHOT of JOE walking toward them)

(JOE enters the scene and looks around. HE sees Flip and heads toward him.)

(FLIP puts up a hand)

> FLIP
> Yo, Joe. Let's talk.
> (JOE crosses to him)

> JOE
> What about?

(FLIP doesn't move from his position. CLOSE-UP on FLIP as he looks Joe over carefully.)

> FLIP
> (Meaningfully) Your future.

> BO
> (Speaking up arrogantly) Yeah, about your future.

(FLIP gives Bo a sharp look, BO retreats behind the bench)

> FLIP
> Shut up, retard. I'm talking to the man. (Changing his tone, his attention is back on Joe) We been lookin' you over, kid.

(PAN IN on JOE who fidgets nervously)

> JOE
> Yeah . . . so?

(CAMERA OPENS on group)      FLIP
> We might find a place for you with the Ravens.
(HE waits for an expected reaction but there is none)

> BLINKY
> Yeah, man, you're lucky. Flip thinks you got what it takes.

(FLIP gives BLINKY a light shove for effect and straightens up as if taking back control)

> FLIP
> Will you shut up while I'm talking?
(HE turns his attention back to JOE)
> No manners, these guys got no manners.
(HE eyes Joe curiously)
> There's an initiation, of course. What do you say?

SOUND OF SCHOOL BELL

> JOE
> (Stalling for time) There's the bell. I don't want to be late for math.

(BLINKY steps forward and gets in Joe's face)

> BLINKY
> (Menacingly) Answer the man.

(BO steps forward and joins BLINKY)

BO
Yeah, answer the man.

(JOE is uncomfortable but he looks directly at FLIP)

JOE
(Hesitantly) I-I eh . . . I want to think about it.
(FLIP looks at him hard then with a slight smile, he says casually)

FLIP
What's to think about? Either you're with us or you're against us. You'd better make up your mind . . . (Menacingly) Now!

(LINDA'S VOICE IS HEARD SHOUTING)

LINDA (VOICE OVER)
Hey, Joey. . . . . . . ..

LONG SHOT OF LINDA RUNNING TOWARD THEM

(SHE comes into the scene and grabs JOE'S hand.
(FLIP steps in front of them to block the way.)

LINDA
(Her attention on Joe) Come on, Joe, you promised me your math homework.
(SHE turns her attention and charm on FLIP who still stands in front of them)
Give me a break, Flip.

(FLIP steps aside.)

LONG SHOT OF JOE AND LINDA RUNNING OFF HAND IN HAND

PAN BACK TO SHOT OF FLIP
(HE stands looking after them and punches his fist in his hand)

FLIP
No manners. That kid's got no manners. I'm gonna have to see he gets some lessons.

CAMERA PANS BACK TO INCLUDE BO AND BLINKY
(THEY nod approvingly)

SOUND OF SCHOOL BELL
FADE OUT

As you can see by the comparison of the two scripts, the screenplay or video gives more directions for the camera and the action. It is focused on the picture, where the stage play is focused on the words. Most schools have video equipment readily available, so that if you decide to use that format, you have an additional job for one of your group, the cameraman. Whichever format your players decide upon, remember "the play's the thing." Shakespeare completed the phrase, "wherein I'll catch the conscience of the King," but a play can catch the conscience of whatever audience it's aimed for.

For young people growing up in communities plagued with poverty, drugs, and violence, schools can be the place to learn nonviolent ways to solve problems and resolve conflicts. Above all they should feel safe. They should develop tolerance for unfamiliar customs and cultures. There is a growing consensus that without addressing social problems, educating young people may be an impossible task. We must provide support and resources to stem the tide of violence before it overwhelms our youth. What better way than to invite them to create their own plays dealing with the issues they're facing in their daily lives? Once you understand how conflict works and how it can be resolved and/or work for you, the easier it is to deal with it in everyday life.

## SUMMARY

All drama is conflict. Without conflict there is no story. Plays have three main components: plot, character, and dialogue. Writing a play is hard work but also an exciting and mind-expanding adventure. Playwriting requires insight into human nature, an understanding of what makes people tick, as well as an understanding of cause and effect. It takes the ability to verbalize thoughts and feelings. Good playwrights are good observers. Professional plays and screenplays are created in collaboration with a variety of different artists. Creating a play with others is a perfect example of cooperative learning. Collaboration is never easy and works best when there is mutual respect among the players; this often means putting aside individual differences for the success of the script. It teaches the participants to listen to others, to accept their ideas, and to weigh the choices offered. Playwriting offers the participants a chance to see the world through someone else's eyes. This process offers them learning in a way that is fun and exciting. In this environment they're not afraid to make a mistake. Acting engages the whole body/self. This drama practice heightens students comprehension of what conflict resolution is all about. The experience offers the added benefit of being self-initiated learning, which involves feelings as well as the intellect.

# 13

## Conflict Resolution in Theatre and Life

The proper study of mankind is man.

*Alexander Pope*

Just as actors learn to create anger in a role, they also learn to control that anger before it turns to rage. Rehearsing different ways to deal with conflict can serve us well. It can teach us how to escalate a situation or how to de-escalate that same problem. Controlling emotions in times of anger is one of the skills we all admire in a good actor's performance. "I thought he was actually going to kill her, he looked so mad!" commented a playgoer after witnessing a production of *Othello*. "And then when I went backstage after the show, they were real lovey-dovey. How can they do that?"

The theatre is a place that portrays these conflicts, of every size, involving any number of people, based on every human emotion, desire, and need. In other words, the theatre is a place to portray every conflict ever imagined or known to man. Of course, the display of emotions is one of actors' primary skills. They train to show the audience exactly what they are feeling through looks, gestures, body language, or whatever else they deem necessary to portray their feelings to the audience. Most actors talk about the *catharsis* they feel after a particularly intense role. Playing a demanding part offers a kind of healing release for the actor. It reflects the foundations of the theatre as a religious and/or healing experience.

## THEATRE FOR HEALING AND
## SOCIAL REFORM

The theatre was recognized as a healing art as far back as Aristotle (384–322 B.C.), who wrote the most influential work on the Greek theatre, the *Poetics,* and Marcus Aurelius (121–180 A.D.), a Roman emperor and writer. Both of these ancient philosophers saw the powerful healing potential in theatre and drama. Records show us that some of the early European asylums had theatre facilities. Between 1797 and 1811 the director of the Charenton Asylum in France worked with patients in theatre productions. The Marquis de Sade (1740–1814) was an inmate in that institution. "By the mid-nineteenth century a number of large asylums were being built with the theatre as part of the main structure" (Jones 1996).

Affirming the healing power of the theatre and drama activities in this country, performances were done back in the 1940s at the Riggs Theatre at Austen Riggs Psychiatric Center in Stockton, Massachusetts. In 1975 they did *The Persecution and Assassination of Jean-Paul Marat as Performed by the Inmates of the Asylum of Charenton Under the Direction of the Marquis de Sade.* The tradition of experimentation in theatre and its acknowledged healing power were important concepts in the development of drama therapy.

Jacob L. Moreno (1889–1974) developed his *Theatre of Spontaneity* in 1921 and continued it until 1923. Here he experimented with ways to make the theatrical experience more meaningful and communal. The actors functioned as social researchers and immersed themselves in the news events of the day. Together the actors and audience created *The Living Newspaper.* Audiences were invited to suggest topics of the day from which the actors would improvise. They would try out various alternative solutions to the problems presented. Out of these early experiments, sociodrama was born. Here the group is the subject, and focuses on a central issue or common concern. Conflict resolution is practiced through the technique of discovering alternative solutions for the problems used for exploration.

Sociodrama came about as an alternative to psychodrama, which deals with personal problems. Both modalities were created by Moreno who saw sociodrama as a way to connect the world community. Moreno stated that all the problems of the world could be solved through sociodrama. This modality for problem solving and conflict resolution is still very popular today and growing in the number of its practitioners. For more information on this modality see *Sociodrama: Who's in Your Shoes?* (Sternberg and Garcia 1989, 10).

In the 1930s and 1940s Bertolt Brecht worked to establish connections between theatre and political change, both in society and in the lives of the individuals attending the theatre. He wrote episodic drama in which he stopped the action with a song, changed plot lines, used short and long scenes and sometimes no scene at all. With these techniques he aimed to have his audience think about what they were looking at. He felt he could affect change in the lives of his performers as well as those in the audiences. These techniques again became popular in the 1960s and 1970s as a number of special interest groups attempted to create changes in the society and bring about social revolution (Wilson 1976).

A new political theatre came about in the 1960s in South America and affirmed for us the potential of drama to change society. In his book *Theatre of the Oppressed* (1979) Augusto Boal stated, "The theatre is a weapon, a very efficient weapon." He would have us remove the barriers between actors and spectators and use theatre as a political forum.

Forum theatre sessions are usually organized by a group of people of similar social origins with a common interest in the resolution of an immediate problem. Sometimes the debate regarding the problem can be as important as resolving the conflict itself. Participants in the forum will be asked to tell a story (it can be a personal one) containing a political or social problem with a difficult, but not impossible, solution. Usually it is a story that presents some kind of oppression that the protagonist can struggle against. After the story is told, the central problem is discussed and clarified for all to understand. A scene will then be improvised based on the story. If the solution proposed is not sufficient to resolve the problem, the audience discusses the action and the scene is performed again. Now, however, any audience member can stop the action at any time and replace the protagonist. This *spect-actor* is given enough time to finish the intervention before any other member can come in with another solution. Each spect-actor intervening in the action must respect the given circumstances of the situation in the scene. He must offer a new solution. He cannot change the socioeconomic circumstances, the family relationships, or the motivation for taking or not taking an action. The purpose of the forum is not necessarily to find an ideal solution but to propose new ways of confronting the oppression. This often serves as a rehearsal for potential decisions in life situations. This type of interactive theatre offers anyone who wishes to participate an opportunity to play the role of problem solver. It also vividly illustrates exactly where the conflicts lie. Forum theatre uses many of the same techniques found in sociodrama.

Boal (1979) sums up the work this way, "Perhaps the theatre is not revolutionary in itself, but it is surely a rehearsal for the revolution." For more information on this technique see *Theatre of the Oppressed* by Augusto Boal.

There are other groups who use sociodrama and forum theatre techniques to explore troublesome issues in the workplace, such as cultural and racial clashes, sexual harassment, hostility toward temporary employees, and difficult coworkers. They set up the conflict and a possible resolution. From there they solicit audience feedback for alternative solutions. Many groups actively involve as many audience members as choose to participate. The scenes are replayed either with a new person playing the problem solver or with the first problem solver repeating her role but using an alternative suggested by the audience. Once again, using this format the conflict is clearly identified and the elements leading up to it pointed out. In the next chapter you will hear from a variety of directors of theatre companies that specialize in theatre for conflict resolution.

The beauty of watching these kinds of performances is the clarity with which the climax can be identified. At that high point of action, the character may have only a few choices. But as you examine the rising action, you discover that there are often many other choices that could have been made at different times that would have led to a different climax.

## THEATRE FOR LIFE SKILLS

Through theatre, students can see and practice a variety of ways that characters respond to stressful emotions in an assortment of situations. When they play a character different from themselves, they have the opportunity to hold a problem up to a mirror and look at it closely. How does that problem change the character? What does he or she go through that brings about growth? Although the change occurs in the fictional character, the actor and the audience both grow through feeling and watching that change. The more ways they learn how to respond to an emotion, the more choices they will have in dealing with those feelings when they occur in life. In other words, when we feel we have more choices available to us, we will meet a variety of situations with the confidence of having "been there" before.

A basic rule of conflict resolution is that the earlier you intervene in a chain of events, the more likely you are to reach a satisfying solution. Identifying a conflict early and predicting problems are basic skills of conflict management. Often effective responses to conflict come from intuition or our own creative imagination instead of from rational thinking. A creative, unexpected action or a new perspective can often defuse a potentially violent situation. Sometimes through this type of intervention we are able to create the possibility of resolution for an apparently intractable conflict.

There are many conflict resolution programs for classroom use, and every teacher has had experience in dealing with discipline problems, some of which lead to violence. An experienced high school teacher named Barry offers this advice: "Students know exactly how to suck you in to their conflicts. And the minute you start to offer a solution, you're hooked. You have added to the problem. Now it's partly your problem and they know it. The only people who can resolve the conflict are the people involved. All you can do is act as a facilitator. Don't let them talk through you, 'She did this and then I did that. . . .' Insist they direct their remarks to each other." A strategy he has found successful in dealing with classroom conflict is to use other students to mediate the dispute. In fact, he keeps a list posted on the bulletin board in the front of the room. He calls his list the Ten Commandments for Conflict Management. He frequently asks the mediator or another student to read the list out loud before the mediation begins.

### DO

1. View the conflict simply as a problem to be solved
2. Direct the participants to face each other but the mediator stands in the middle.
3. Direct the participants to talk to each other (not the mediator).
4. Ask questions. ("What's going on here?" "What's the problem?" )

5. Listen actively to each person. Let them know you understand what they're saying. ("Do I understand correctly that you hit him because. . . .")
6. Identify the problem.
7. Ask for more specific information.
8. Encourage the participants to try to solve their own problem reasonably.
9. Acknowledge possible solutions offered.
10. Acknowledge their feelings.

### DON'T

1. Buy into the problem or become judgmental. ("Why did you say that?")
2. Become the enforcer or threaten punishment.
3. Solve the problem or rescue one of the participants.

"We like to practice beforehand also, and we make up different scenarios where they set up the problems. We stop them just before they get hot and let the mediator take over."

The four short scripts below work well for this exercise. The dialogue sets up a problem and the players improvise it beyond the scripted lines and take it as far as they choose before the mediator calls "cut!" Then the mediator takes over and practices the ten commandments above to see if the players can be helped to settle their differences. The actors stay in role during the mediation. They don't always find a solution for these problems, but the practice is what counts. Learning how to ask the right questions in settling a dispute is also a valuable lesson. With this kind of practice it's easier to remember how to proceed when the real thing happens.

### Script # 1

# 1: Don't just sit there, do something!
# 2: What do you want me to do?
# 1: I don't care! Just do something.
# 2: Tell me what to do, and I'll do it.
# 1: You're only making it worse.
# 2: What am I doing?
# 1: Stop it right now or I'll start throwing something.
# 2: (Improvise from here) _____

### Script # 2

\# 1: You did it again!

\# 2: What? What did I do?

\# 1: You know very well what you did, and I'm sick and tired of it.

\# 2: I don't know what you're talking about.

\# 1: It's always the same thing with you. Lie! Lie! Lie!

\# 2: Now you're calling me names. Cut it out.

\# 1: I'll call you anything I please. You're a no good—

\# 2: _____

### Script # 3

\# 1: You'd better stop right now or I'll scream.

\# 2: Are you crazy?

\# 1: Don't try to put the blame on me.

\# 2: What's the matter with you?

\# 1: I'm warning you if you don't stop I'll scream.

\# 2: Stop what?

\# 1: I warned you. You'll be sorry—

\# 2: _____

### Script # 4

\# 1: You'd better leave now.

\# 2: Why?

\# 1: You'd just better go, that's all.

\# 2: What if I don't want to?

\# 1: I said I want you to leave.

\# 2: No, I'm not leaving.

\# 1: I said, get out now!

\# 2: _____

Remind your mediator to review the Ten Commandments for Conflict Management before the scene starts. Ask your actors to stay in character, to continue their roles in the conflict even after their improvisation is cut, while the mediator asks them questions. Review the situation as if it were a real conflict occurring between the players.

## THEATRE FOR SELF-UNDERSTANDING

The principal of a large urban high school put it this way, "Prevention programs are far more effective when they teach a core of emotional and social competencies, such as impulse control, anger management, reducing prejudices, and finding creative solutions to social predicaments. The thing is we all have choices about how we respond to emotions. You and I have been taught a variety of acceptable ways to respond, but all these kids know is violence. We need to give them more practice for living skills."

This brings us right back to using theatre skills in the classroom as a method for conflict resolution, anger management, and better self-understanding. In his book *Development Through Drama*, Brian Way tells us that students need to develop an awareness of emotions and self. He points out that "no two people are alike not only in physical appearance but in emotions and imagination, which comprise the root of individuality" (Way 1967).

Self-awareness is the first step the adolescent must reach in order to be an effective problem solver and decision maker, which in turn will give him more self-esteem. With this self-awareness young people can learn how to maintain self-control. The crucial factor here is to point out that we always have *choices* in how we respond to emotion. However, if we have experienced only one way and are unwilling to learn other methods, there is no choice. Within your examination of emotions, help your players learn to acknowledge what they're feeling. Discuss it. Label it. When they feel overpowered, direct them to take a deep breath and say the line, "I am in control. I decide whether to accept or reject this emotion." Point out that the emotion is a force that is trying to take control of the person at the moment. No one wants to be out of control.

## RIGHT WAY/WRONG WAY

For a quick look at a broad variety of conflict resolution in everyday life, tune in to a soap opera. Here's an exercise your players will like. Ask them to watch their favorite soap opera for several days and keep a conflict log on it. The lessons offered in these TV stories illustrate dramatic examples of *right way/wrong way* techniques for conflict resolution—with plenty of emotion thrown in. Direct your players to keep a list of the conflicts. Use three columns across. Jot down the conflict in the first column. Label the column right next to it *Right Way* and the other *Wrong Way*. The conflict should be listed in the first column and then the students should check the column in which they think the conflict falls. Was it handled correctly or incorrectly? Below the conflict make a note of overlooked alternatives. Which incidents were the precursors to the major conflict and the final climax? Which ones could have been resolved so that the problem wouldn't escalate? Which were caused by a threat or challenge to ego, respect, or a rekindling of past grievances? What problems were magnified by low self-esteem?

For future playwrights, this exercise offers an interesting study not only of conflict resolution but of dramatic structure as well. Make a list of the characters in the scene and describe the conflict style of each. How did the character's conflict style contribute to the problem? Which characters used each style: Fight, flight, or communicate? Did any of them overcome their anger or violent tendencies by acting calm even though they weren't?

## NEGOTIATOR GAME

This is a game that offers in-the-scene experience that will help your actors become more aware of their own conflict triggers and conflict style while also offering excellent practice for the future playwrights in the group. In addition, this activity promotes understanding of self and others, helping your actors learn more about themselves and their behavior. As Cervantes tells us, know thyself, which is the most difficult lesson in the world.

You'll select two players to begin their argument using the scripts below. Another player will function as the *negotiator* who will come up with a line when the director calls "now!" The purpose of the negotiator's line is to break the tension or de-escalate the actor's anger. There is no one line or single approach that works all the time. What this game does is to help the actor playing the negotiator to think on her feet and illustrate to other players that there are ways to step into a conflict and become the negotiator. (Granted, some are safer than others and you'll pick your interventions carefully.)

Before you begin the scenes, brainstorm some possible intervention lines for the negotiator. For example, some intervention lines might include the following.

1. Whoaaa, horse! Slow down.
2. Stop . . . (and sing the next line) in the name of love.

3. Hey, wait a minute, there's Madonna (Brad Pitt, or any current celebrity).
4. Cut! Start over again like it's fun and I'll film it.
5. Help! I'm going to throw up. Where's the bathroom?
6. How do you feel about abortion?
7. How do you feel about legalizing marijuana?
8. Excuse me, I'm taking a poll. How do you feel about lowering the voting age to sixteen?
9. Excuse me, I'm taking a poll. How do you feel about year-round school?
10. Excuse me, I'm taking a poll. How do you feel about mandatory military service?

Keep a list of the ones your players come up with for future reference and review them before you start the game. You may want to put them on the board so that the negotiator has easy and quick access to the lines.

### Scene #1 (for two males)

#1: Get outa my face, man!
#2: You talkin' to me, jerk?
#1: Yeah, I'm talkin' to you, *jerk*. Get outa my way.
#2: Who's gonna make me?
**DIRECTOR: Now!**

At this point the actor assigned the negotiator role speaks a line that he feels may de-escalate or break the tension. The negotiator lines listed below are some that came up in working with a high school group:

Hey, fellows look over there, isn't that Madonna?
Excuse me, I'm taking a poll on anger. Could you tell me what you're mad about?
Cut! Okay guys, try it again like you're having fun, and we'll film it.
I need two guys to sample the new candy bar. You interested?
Excuse me, but where's the bathroom?
Hey, guys, come on. They're giving away free pizza and sodas in the cafeteria.

### Scene #2 (for two females)

#1: You been comin' on to my man.
#2: So what you gonna do about it?
#1: Stay away or I'll show you.
#2: Let's see you try it!
**DIRECTOR: Now!**
NEGOTIATOR: _____

Hold it! I'm a talent scout, and you two would be great for my
next movie
Hey, look over there, isn't that Brad Pitt?
Excuse me, but where's the ladies room?
Look out, here comes the principal.
Wow! This is a great scene for my new movie. But what if he
dumps both of you and you become best friends?

### Scene #3 (one male and one female)

#1: Nobody dumps me.
#2: No, well I did.
#1: How 'd you like a punch in the mouth.
#1: Try it!
**DIRECTOR: Now!**
NEGOTIATOR : _____

The best negotiator lines will come from your players themselves.
Let everyone take a turn at coming up with a negotiator line. Never
underestimate the power of humor in these situations or of the
lines that seem to put the antagonists off balance such as the last
one in scene two. Some lines may be silly and others may not really
deal with the situation, but the discussion, exploration, and discovery of the lines that do work are what counts here. The great
ancient Roman philosopher and playwright Seneca tells us, "The
greatest remedy for anger is delay." Which lines interrupt the
action just long enough to de-escalate the anger? Obviously, tone
of voice and the manner in which the line was delivered played a
part in the successful interventions, and different lines worked better with some people than with others. An important objective of
this game, then, is to discover which lines work best with your

group and under what circumstances. Once again the process here is more important than the product.

Another behavior that the game encourages is for the negotiator to stay calm or act calm when he steps into a conflict. This technique is practiced by most anger management specialists. There is a saying among substance abusers who are in recovery, "Fake it, till you make it." In other words, if you can learn to play the role of a calm person even when you don't feel that way, you can successfully navigate through a potentially violent situation when it erupts in life. Once again we turn to the theatre to play the role we want to project rather than the one we might be feeling at the moment.

Bryar Cougle, arts education consultant for the North Carolina public schools, gives us an overview of the concepts taught and learned through the theatre arts. Just a few that he lists are leadership, teamwork, discipline, dedication, pride in the work, responsibility, self-esteem, and conflict resolution, which includes problem recognition and problem solving. His list of skills that students learn include how to communicate, interact with others, compromise, achieve, and understand and apply basic principles of logic and argument. In addition, he believes the theatre teaches its participants to "mentally fly—to go beyond everyday thinking." Let us inspire all our participants to immerse themselves in the theatre arts, so they learn not only theatre for conflict resolution but also to go beyond everyday thinking, to "mentally fly" as well.

## SUMMARY

The theatre is built on conflict. Without it there is no drama. The theatre has long been recognized for its healing power, as far back as Aristotle and Marcus Aurelius. Jacob L. Moreno developed his *Theatre of Spontaneity* in 1921; the actors functioned as social researchers and focused on the group's common concern or central issue. Moreno saw this modality of sociodrama as a way to connect the world community. That premise of group problem solving offers a model for conflict resolution. The theatre offers a platform for self-discovery and understanding. Two theatre artists who have used the theatre to promote change in society are Bertolt Brecht and Augusto Boal. Brecht felt he could affect change in the life of his performers as well as those in the audience. Indeed, he saw the power of drama to examine the human condition and promote new ways of thinking. Another theatre that examines social and political problems is forum theatre made famous by Augusto Boal. Most often it focuses on a story that presents some oppression that the protagonist can struggle against. This type of theatre uses many of the same techniques found in sociodrama. Numerous conflict resolution groups practice techniques similar to those found in these modalities. (See Chapter 14 for examples.) Play productions and dramatic literature offer opportunities to study conflict and conflict styles, as well as techniques by which those conflicts can be resolved without resorting to violence. We can learn from actors to interrupt anger long enough to de-escalate a situation and to do so while remaining calm ourselves. Theatre and drama promote self-esteem by offering the participants practice in handling many different roles in a variety of life situations. The theatre has been holding up a mirror to our society as long as people have been around to write about problems or act them out. We may not find all the answers through our work in theatre and drama, but we can become more aware of the questions to ask, and we can practice a variety of positive behaviors to deal with all types of conflicts. At the very least our rehearsal in drama for life situations will equip us to understand ourselves and others and arm us to deal with many of the conflicts that are part of everyday life in today's world.

"Curtain going up!"

# 14

# Who's Doing What

There's nothing like a dream to create the future.
*Victor Hugo*

It's not possible to identify all the groups who use conflict resolution and problem-solving scripts in their theatre productions, so a sampling of companies and their various approaches and philosophical underpinnings are offered here. The groups selected are either known to me or were recommended. Some groups work directly with youngsters in creating their own plays, while others focus on the artistic aesthetic and offer professional theatre productions. Some groups work interactively with audiences. Most of these theatres offer workshops, classroom activities, or study guides for further experience and learning after the performance. All of them believe in the power of drama/theatre and its ability to change lives.

Diana Feldman, founder and executive director of ENACT, explains her philosophy this way: "My underlying philosophy has always remained the same. It is the belief that everyone is born with a divine nature and given a different set of obstacles and circumstances to work through in order for that nature to emerge. The ENACT work helps students work through the obstacles that interfere with their personal growth and potential. We try to provide them with opportunities for creative expression in the hope that they may discover or glimpse their own divinity, which is unique and has different expressions for each individual."

That belief in creativity is shared by Denise Boston-Moore, director of Creative Visions. She says, "Knowledge is power. Creativity ignites knowledge that lies within. Children have the innate ability to transform their experiences and move confidently within the unknown. Environmental settings that promote artistic expression allow children and youth the opportunity to sculpt powerful images and weave passionate stories, to resolve conflicts, render solutions to personal and global problems, and appreciate the value of life."

Each of these theatre groups provide drama/theatre for conflict resolution. Some take their work a step further and focus on global issues in violence prevention.

## CITY AT PEACE
Paul Griffin, Director
Written by Paul Griffin, Elizabeth Segal, and Elly Kugler

City at Peace, located in Washington, DC, is an intense program that involves as many as 70 young people for a full year to create an original musical based on their lives, which is focused on violence prevention. Violence is interpreted broadly to include domestic abuse and neglect, self-inflicted violence, and social violence, as in racial, economic, or sexual prejudice. In fact, participants are encouraged to share their lives and to develop a script that reflects the issues their stories raise.

The program began in DC in 1989, with about 30 young people, directed by Carlo Grossman and Rickey Payton [composer and music director] and produced by Rosey Simonds. It grew out of an international program called Peace Child, initially created to deal with U. S.-Soviet relations by providing an opportunity for children to have a voice about their future.

The Washington program, under Paul Griffin's direction since 1994, begins in May with about 100 youth (13-19 years) from city and suburban, alternative and independent schools and special programs. Noncompetitive "auditions" are held to introduce students and their parents on what to expect.

Saturday rehearsals include warm-ups, development or basic agreements, plus structured games and improvisation. Group agreements include confidentiality, amnesty (allowing people room to change), and striving to maintain respect for other's comfort levels while challenging one's own. After the group begins to gel, members tell their life stories in a ten-minute answer to the question "What makes you who you are?" Out of these stories a script is created. Using improvisation and writing, small groups sculpt their stories into theatrical form. Vocal, dance, and theatre training are ongoing, with a music director and a choreographer coming in for blocks of time.

A production team of ten second-year cast members (chosen by the team from the year before) work in tandem with the director to plan and sometimes conduct rehearsals, make script suggestions, and act as listeners for cast members who are struggling with conflicts at home or school. Participants are not cast in their own stories to preserve confidentiality.

A major performance takes place in November with the aid of a technical director who manages, with youth assistants, lights, sound, and any set that may be used. This performance is a major fund-raising event, with individual and corporate donations providing blocks of free tickets for high school groups. The following months' performance in schools, conferences, and events keep the group busy and broaden their horizons.

Commitment is developed over time and out of choice, not by contract. Amnesty for missing rehearsals is granted for family events and school work. However, participants are held responsible for informing the director in advance. Students are encouraged to plan ahead so they can make the additional rehearsals as production time approaches—and they do.

Paul and the cast are constantly making connections between the demands of City at Peace and life. "If you don't show up for life you miss the action." As the performance demonstrates, the program is about transforming lives, and it works for those who stick with it. Some who have come back two and three years later will say, "I didn't really get it until I left." The support of the group is what makes the difference for participants. And what a difference it is making, bringing the lessons of hope and understanding created by youth, for youth, for the future and to our community.

## CREATIVE VISIONS
Denise Boston-Moore, Director

I am a witness to the power and effectiveness of imaginative expression. As an arts educator, the population that I have worked with primarily has been urban African American children and adolescents. Together we transform classrooms, recreational facilities, and church basements into sacred spaces where everyone's thoughts, dreams, and wishes come to life. Within this environment African American children have the opportunity to step away from daily stressors (drugs, violence, hunger, poverty) and experience safety, creativity, and fun. A world of socially imposed inhibitors seriously undermines the creative genius of African American children.

I have served as program director for several arts organizations in the Washington, DC, and Baltimore metropolitan areas over the past twenty years. In the latter part of the 1970s, with the escalation of youth-related violent crimes in the African American community, I saw a need to develop artistic programs the emphasized creative ways for managing conflict and impulsive behavior. My concentration is on providing workshops, classes, and lectures to organizations and agencies that work with individuals struggling with barriers and obstacles (i.e., poverty, illiteracy, adjudication, drug addiction, racism, mental illness). I firmly believe that by exposing organizations and agencies to the effectiveness of expressive arts, more people will understand the concept of social change through the use of creative programs. Artistic expression is liberating. It stimulates people into action and action into positive results.

To do this creative work requires a clear understanding of the problems African Americans face in this society. In the inner-cities, so much depends on how African American youth view their limitations and unpredictable existences. Without respect, love, and positive reinforcement, many of them have been left alone to create negative and self-destructive situations. In order for the creative process to make a difference in their lives, it is crucial to apply a system that is relevant to their cultural and social world.

I understand the environmental factors of children and families that I work with, because I have lived in their neighborhoods as well. I was neighbor to families who exemplified strength and dignity. I saw mothers, fathers, and grandparents holding on and struggling to rear their children despite the deficiencies and devastation of oppressive living conditions. I use improvisation, poetry, and movement to address everything that comes out of this environment; the hope as well as the desolation. In our classes and workshops we create worlds where children are in control, where injustice and hatred are eradicated, and where everyone has a purpose. This work has produced awesome results and precious moments. I have been inspired and moved by the tenacity of African American youth.

Creativity in the form of music, visual arts, dance, or drama is the key to broadening one's perspective of life and the people around them. Each art modality offers individuals an opportunity to understand on a deeper level how essential the arts are in their lives. My work links imagination and a sociocultural frame of reference in order to gain a fuller clarification of the nature of the African American child's social universe. I firmly believe that an affirming and creative environment is the key to optimum growth and development. As artists, we now have the data and research that supports the position that creative experiences, even under the most constrained of circumstances, has the power to transform images.

## THE CREATIVE ARTS TEAM
Chris Vine, Director

The Creative Arts Team is one of the oldest and the largest professional theatre-in-education companies in the USA. For more than twenty years it has been pioneering the use of interactive theatre and drama techniques to help young people address current curricular themes and explore relevant contemporary social issues; high on its list of priorities has been a continuing commitment to conflict resolution.

The original inspiration for CAT came from the related British practices of process-oriented drama-in-education (DIE) and performance based theatre-in-education (TIE), which emerged during the late sixties and early seventies. A second significant, if slightly later source of influence was the work of Augusto Boal and his system of participatory theatre known as the Theatre of the Oppressed. Drama is best suited to challenge predetermined value systems. Rather than presenting answers, it is better suited to raising questions, exploring alternatives, and finding new meanings.

The influences from these different traditions are still central to the development of CAT's work today, but have been supplemented by other influences and challenges arising from the specific social and cultural contexts in which the work takes place. This is particularly well exemplified by CAT's evolving approach to conflict resolution and the peculiar development of that strand in its work.

Because of the prevalence of conflict, and traditions of extreme violence in American society, particularly in urban settings, it was inevitable and appropriate that at an early stage in its development CAT should become involved in conflict work with young people, and thereby enter into a new phase of cross-fertilization between its own educational theatre processes and the growing body of theory and practice in the field of conflict resolution.

CAT swiftly developed models of practice that enabled young people to examine conflict in fictional situations. It retained its adherence to the use of character and plot and, unlike some other agencies, did not entirely *personalize* the circumstances in which students were asked to explore the alternative actions that might avoid or defuse conflict. In other words, students were asked to act *on behalf of,* or *as if* they were, other people—that is, the characters they met through the drama.

Another variation of our work , usually targeted on junior high and high school students, examine conflicts embedded in the complexities of everyday life. These problems are approximated in a traditional performance format as original full-scale dramas performed to much larger audiences in school auditoriums or other theatre venues. This experience was supplemented by in-class workshops with smaller groups of students. All of these models, with variations, are still current in CAT's work.

Learning from other professionals in the conflict field, CAT developed some simple paradigms to provide structure in its work and provide a focus for students. These included a practical step model for approaching conflicts and a decision-making sequence to encourage students to identify their possible choices, and consider likely consequences, before deciding how they might act. Identify *choices* › consider *consequences* › make informed *decisions.*

Boal insists that if we want to change our actions, be it to combat the oppression of others, violent or otherwise, or our own habitual responses, we have to be able to see the larger picture. In that way we can begin to understand needs and motives, and identify those moments when we can make a different choice, before events run out of control.

Acting upon these many concerns, Gwendolen Hardwick, the director of the CAT High School Program, developed a new project using a nonnaturalistic presentation incorporating stylized movement, masks, a sound collage (including contemporary music and lyrics familiar to the students), "sick" humor, and physical still images, the students were encouraged to create their own definitions of violence—and begin debating them. The new work-shop sequence was entitled *In Our Own Voice*.

One of the central themes that emerges time after time from the lives of the young students we encounter is their own sense of worthlessness and lack of power. Too often the negative situations under scrutiny in the work only serve to reinforce this viewpoint. For this reason it was decided to move forward in time and add an epilogue to the story, through which the central character could reveal how she has managed to break the cycle of violence and fail-ure, and put her life back on track. We did not want to manufac-ture a magic happy ending, but felt it was essential to reflect the possibility of change and success without minimizing the commit-ment and effort it requires.

Parallel to these developments, two other programs were also evolving new practices. One of these was the CAT Early Learning Program. This program works with children in pre-K through grade one. During this same period CAT's newest and fastest grow-ing program was its Parent Program. This had grown out of a small amount of previous work designed to encourage parents to support the schooling of their children.

Purists might say that CAT's recent work is too broad in scope to any longer fit within the definition of conflict resolution. Perhaps CAT's work in this arena would be more accurately described as conflict analysis and emotions management. But regardless of labels, the company remains committed to an holistic educational approach that locates individual action within a social framework and invokes both individual and group responsibility.

## ENACT
Diana Feldman, Founder and Executive Director

ENACT is a not-for-profit professional arts-in-education company that has successfully worked in the New York City schools for more than ten years. Our approach, which combines performing arts and drama therapy techniques, facilitates the personal and interper-sonal growth for students of all ages and abilities. We have reached more than 20,000 students, teachers, and parents with our interac-tive drama programs.

Professional actors and therapists work together in classrooms (often special education classes) to create an environment in which optimal learning can take place. Our programs are tailored to meet the specific needs of our students, yet underpinning our work is a focus on self-awareness and responsibility. Programs include conflict resolution through drama (high school and junior high); drama in the classroom (elementary-school aged); and programs designed for students with special needs (autism, physically challenged). Sessions last forty-five minutes, twice a week, for weeks, months, or years depending on the need of the school and the students. Questionnaires are given to teachers ahead of time to help us shape initial lessons around the needs and concerns of the students.

Theatre games and various forms of role-play techniques allow students to "rehearse for life" and work through their obstacles. Instructors encourage thoughts, feelings, and beliefs to be regularly examined and linked to behavior. Alternate positive behaviors are identified and students are made aware of their power to choose and take responsibility for their actions. Students are assisted in making conscious changes in their behavior. The ENACT method results in attitudinal change because we address the causes underlying behavior. While social issues are examined such as peer pressure, substance abuse, teen pregnancy, personal belief systems are given a forum for discussion and evaluation.

In our conflict resolution workshops, we teach practical coping skills such as responsible communication and relaxation techniques. Students are taught how to manage their feelings by becoming aware of them before they act them out. From time to time programs culminate in performances with students and ENACT actors for the additional purpose of bridging gaps with the community and heightening awareness.

A great deal of our work takes place in inner-city schools with students considered "at risk" because of their behavior and extremely low attendance records. ENACT has had great success with these students because our conflict-resolution programs reach them on levels that touch their feelings and acknowledge their sense of individuality. There is no doubt that drama is a powerful tool to elicit human identification. ENACT has the opportunity to employ and train skilled actors, who are able to reflect back realistically and powerfully, aspects of student's behavior in the characters they play. Role plays are selected carefully from our repertoire and shaped according to the needs of the class.

The ENACT method first emerged when I began working with autistic students. When the company began, I was hired to work in special education schools with students who, we were told, could not be reached. Through theatre games, imaginary journeys, music, and movement, various parts of themselves could be expressed. While we shaped our activities, we also learned what emotional protection meant. Only when students felt safe and ready would they let go of their protective devices (often highly creative)and allow other parts of themselves to emerge.

ENACT also brings workshops to parents and teachers helping them work through their own concerns. In this way we form a support system for our work with the students. ENACT also adapts its techniques to other clientele. We have done workshops in hospitals, day treatment centers and corporations. We have brought culminating performances to public arenas locally and present nationally at education and drama therapy conferences. Interns from New York University and Hunter College have worked with our program along with high school interns and volunteers.

## PERIWINKLE NATIONAL THEATRE
Sunna Rasch, Executive Director

The Periwinkle National Theatre was conceived in 1963 in an effort to present exceptional theatre programs that meet student and curriculum needs. Over the past few decades, Periwinkle's work has focused on social issues relevant to the needs and lives of children and youth. Our plays set the stage to examine alternative possibilities and spark an audience's emotions to question human behavior—their own and others. The theatre experience itself primes the audience for participation in the conflict resolution workshops because the students identify with characters in the play. From the beginning our credo stands, *"To unlock a mind, you must first open a heart."*

Although Periwinkle's plays can stand alone as theatre, they go far beyond the theatre experience in their ability to open dialogue and make positive impact on young minds. In each instance, the plays act as a springboard for workshop follow-up. The method is successful because children have already found the auditorium a safe environment to view a professional play on social issues, behavior, and choices that have direct bearing on their own young lives.

These plays focus on a variety of social issues such as drug prevention (*Halfway There*), violence reduction (*Rooftop*), abduction prevention (*Little Red Riding Hood Finds the Safety Zone*), and divorce and an alcoholic parent (*Split Decision*)—all factors that have proven disruptive to a child's sense of self and attitude towards learning.

Our play, *Rooftop*, is for grades 3, 4, 5. *Rooftop* was specifically created by playwright Scott Laughead, also Periwinkle's Director of Education, to address the problem of child-on-child violence. It was created with Stop the Violence funding from the New York City Mayor's office.

Following each performance of the play, the Periwinkle performers are available to conduct hands-on workshops on alternate ways to resolve conflict. The actors split up in teams depending on the number of workshops requested. The workshops begin with a short question-and-answer period about the play and the characters, after which the actors enact a scene from a student selected problem. The students then get involved by stepping into the roles and performing scenarios that can be stopped at any time by the leader. Input from class members provides solutions to the problems. Role playing becomes a strong focus of the workshops as children engage in improvisation of various scenarios that could happen.

All scripts are created by observing children in social situations, mostly in school environments. Periwinkle's emphasis over the past decade has been to commission playwrights to create plays that illustrate strong conflicts with which children can identify and empathize. In its scripts, characters grapple with conflict and employ various tactics currently employed in conflict resolution strategies. These consist of stopping arguments when feelings get too heated, and finding alternative solutions through performance. Trying out these solutions afterward in workshops complete The Periwinkle Experience.

Blending theatre and education brings special gratification to those who make this a life career. Not only do young audiences get exposed to theatre on an arts level—but positive impact for living is made on young lives. If we want to change the world, we must start with the children.

I happen to think that conflict resolution workshops coming out of a theatre experience produce gains that are powerful and effective. In fact, I believe if conflict resolution techniques were *mandatory curriculum for every child*, we would be on our way to improving the atmosphere in schools and ultimately the world.

## RAVES (KAISER PERMANTE)
Martha Johns, Director

Kaiser Permante, a not-for-profit health maintenance organization, has been producing high quality educational theatre for school and community audiences since 1984. Using professional actor-educators, our programs tour daily throughout our service areas. There are seven touring companies nationwide in Northern and Southern California; the Pacific Northwest; Denver, Colorado; Atlanta, Georgia; Cleveland, Ohio; and the Mid-Atlantic States. All our programs are designed to empower young people and adults to make healthy choices in their lives. Using theatre we are able to affect people on an emotional/affective level as well as through cognitive approaches. Active decision making is an essential focus in these "dramatic messages."

RAVES, which stands for Real Alternatives to Violence for Every Student, arose out of evaluative research conducted on our other plays. Elementary schools that had been regular audiences for our popular health and safety plays *Professor Bodywise and the Traveling Menagerie,* told us that violence prevention was as important a health and safety issue as bicycle safety, substance abuse prevention, or nutrition and exercise. This realization caused us to conduct more research on the types of conflicts that were escalating into violence in the schools. Three hundred schools throughout the Mid-Atlantic region were surveyed representing widely divergent demographics. The survey results revealed that the types of conflicts fell into three broad categories around which we scripted our RAVES play. Interestingly enough, the basic issues were the same in kindergarten as in twelfth grade. Only the intensity and expression of the conflicts changed. Those issues included:

1. Personal space/personal properties issues
2. "He said/she said" or reputation issues
3. Lack of understanding about differences: cultural, racial, gender, and handicaps

In each of the three acts of RAVES, a conflict escalates to the point of violence and is then *frozen.* The actor-educators, trained in improvisation, take the students' brainstormed suggestions and create an ending for the scene. RAVES, which uses music and humor, is highly interactive and plays to the entire elementary school. The play serves as a segue to a presentational skills training session conducted by the five actor-educators.

Learning theory tells us that skills not practiced are less likely to be retained. To give students an opportunity to practice their new skills we do two things: First, they are given a set of playing cards with each of the tools explained on them. These include "I" messages, needs statements, apologies, deep breathing exercises, brainstorming techniques for handling put-downs. Between the second and third sessions, students are asked to try the skills on the cards in their daily lives and come back with experiences about how well the skills worked in different situations. Second, during our third day with the students they have an opportunity to do guided role play in a game we call Encounters. Students are the pieces on the board as they negotiate a school day. We find this technique very effective in changing the *culture* in a school where third-party pressure had previously encouraged students in conflict to fight. Finally, during a stage in which skills are owned and consolidated, the elementary students work with trained high school mentors to create a Legacy Project. This is a long-term arts project that uses the visual or performing arts to communicate "The Vision and Value of a Peaceful Community" to the younger students in the school. In this way, the older students take ownership for their position as role models for the entire student body.

Research on RAVES has demonstrated that the whole program is significantly more than the sum of its parts. The total program has been demonstrated to reduce significantly or totally eliminate suspensions for fighting, health room referrals from conflicts, and classroom disruption due to conflict.

## SEEDS OF PEACE
Barbara Gottschalk, Executive Vice President

Seeds of Peace is an independent American program, which brings together delegations of young teenagers from opposing sides of conflict areas in the world, to study conflict areas in the world, to study conflict resolution and experience coexistence in the highly supportive environment of a summer camp in Maine. Founded in 1993 by John Wallach, a noted journalist and author, the primary focus during its first five years has been on the conflict between

Israel, Palestine, and other Arab states. More than 700 young people from all over the Middle East have graduated from Seeds of Peace. They are now bringing the possibility of peace message to their communities, even in the face of overwhelming political shifts away from the peace process. In the 1997 session, 164 teenagers from Israel, Palestine, Egypt, Jordan, Morocco, Tunisia, Qatar, and the United States participated.

Seeds of Peace is unique as the only program that brings together youngsters from 11 countries in the Arab world that have peace agreements with Israel and Israelis in an overnight camp setting. Here they experience structured group workshops on communication and coexistence skills. It is the only program that builds a network of youth throughout the Middle East. Together they write a newspaper and are connected by lasting friendships through letters, e-mail, faxes, art projects, weekend retreats, telephone calls, and visits. Most important, it is the only program of its kind that has the full confidence and publicly-demonstrated respect of the political leaders all over the world.

As United Nations Secretary-General Kofi Annan has said, "There can be no more important initiative than bringing together young people who have seen the ravages of war to learn the art of peace. Seeds of Peace is certainly an example of the world the United Nations is actively working for."

Seeds of Peace stresses violence prevention and relationship building, not only between individuals, but also in the community context. The mission is to train the next generation of leaders for living together in peace, using conflict resolution strategies, along with an actual experience of living in peace in a neutral territory. The counselors who live with the youngsters are educated in conflict resolution as well as in camp skills. They do not just teach swimming or boating or baseball, they also monitor the way the mixed-national teams interact with each other. They pair up campers from opposing sides of the conflict, to depend on each other, to achieve a common goal, and to form bonds. Campers are expected to speak English, the acknowledged language at camp, so that all utterances are understood by everyone within earshot.

The daily Coexistence Workshops, led by professional facilitators, utilize many forms of communication, including interactive drama, sensitivity games, group-building activities, oral history skills, listening and debating skills, music, art, and discussion. By teaching youngsters effective conflict resolution techniques in an atmosphere that fosters mutual respect and understanding. Seeds of Peace staff and alumni continue to work with the participants after they return to their countries. Seeds of Peace helps them become the seeds from which enduring peace has a chance to grow. As one graduate has stated, "Seeds of Peace is where you find out what kind of character you really have." It is a lesson for a lifetime.

## STOP-GAP THEATRE
Don R. Laffoon, Cofounder and Executive Director

Good theatre means *drama,* and there is no drama without conflict. Conflict is what fuels the drama. Without drama, theatre is dead. But when we allow this kind of drama to fuel our lives, we can end up hurting ourselves and others. Disagreement becomes anger, becomes rage, becomes death.

In real life, on the mean streets of Los Angeles, and on too many school campuses in cities large and small, the spilled blood is real. The curtain never goes back up for Joe or Jose. The darkness is real. The applause is replaced by the sound of weeping. A mother cries for a son, and a brother cries out for revenge.

So, how does one put "conflict resolution" on the stage and make it engaging? If you make your hero the person who walks away from a fight, student audiences are likely to find him or her boring. We educators need to follow young people's advice and "get real." Whose actions are more interesting, Gandhi's or Schwarzenegger's? Rosa Park's or Xena, the Warrior Princess'? Nelson Mandela's or Mike Tyson's (both in the ring and out of it)?

We at STOP-GAP feel deeply committed to the idea of using the theatre to focus on ways of resolving conflict, and we approach it from two directions: prevention and intervention. Some of us remember our childhood when a parent read or told us a story that we didn't want to end. Maybe we need better stories or perhaps we need to tell stories better.

In the area of intervention, each week we conduct five drama therapy sessions with adolescent drug addicts at the Phoenix House; young adult runaways, seeking shelter in downtown Hollywood; pregnant teens in a school-based program in Long Beach; and children at the county shelter for victims of physical, sexual, and emotional abuse. These young lives are filled with conflict, filled with drama. Without proper intervention, they will continue to play the roles into which they have been cast: victim and victimizer. Through role-plays and other drama therapy techniques, STOP-GAP allows them to identify and then shed old roles.

STOP-GAP is equally committed to prevention: at least five of our twelve plays that tour to classrooms throughout Southern California are related to conflict resolution. They are *Acting your R/AGE!, You Decide!, Same Difference, Killer Pain,* and *An I for An Eye for An Aye.* *An I for An Eye* is about looking someone in the eye instead of punching them in the eye. It's about going for the "Aye," the yes, the win/win so that *I* stay safe and nobody has to lose.

*Killer Pain* investigates conflict within our families and ourselves, and how some of us turn to alcohol and other drugs as a way to run away from the hurt. We know what the pain killers are (alcohol and other drugs). Our play is an interactive theatre approach in searching for the Killer Pain. *Same Difference* is an interactive presentation that explores what makes people seem different and to experience what makes them the same. *You Decide!* is about decision making and the consequences for actions. The scripted portion follows the story of Marty, who always lets other people decide for him. In the interactive section, the classroom audience gets to teach Marty how to make decisions that are healthy for *him*. *Acting Your R/AGE!*, as the title suggests, is about whether we are indeed acting in a mature and thoughtful way or acting out some internal rage.

All of STOP-GAP's classroom presentations tend to ask the following two questions: Where is the hurt? Where is the help? Once we identify the hurt, we can begin to seek out help.

Yes, I have spent my life in the theatre: from a ten-year-old with a magic act (not great) and touring puppet show (pretty darn good) to cofounding STOP-GAP in 1979. I have learned that I am at my best when I keep the drama *on* the stage and *out* of my personal and professional lives. Conflict will always exist in life, but it is our choice whether or not we make it into drama. The apparent contradiction between theatre and conflict resolution is resolved when we realize that we need to return the drama to the stage where it belongs.

The companies mentioned here show us many ways that drama and theatre connect people and ideas. They show us how theatre is used as a place where problems can be solved and violence controlled. Theatre offers a symbolic safe place, a nonjudgmental environment, and an aesthetic distance for exploring any of life's problems or conflicts. What better place to practice the skills of conflict resolution than in the theatre. Trust yourself and the work. Drama serves as a means to revitalize people of all ages and especially young people. It can be that bridge to reconnect our adolescents to the possibilities that life has to offer. Theatre broadens their world. It opens their eyes to the possibilities in life and helps them acquire skills to make those possibilities become reality.

# References

AMERICAN ASSOCIATION OF SCHOOL ADMINISTRATORS. 1995. *Conflict Resolution: Learning to Get Along.* Arlington, VA: MSA.

BANKS, JAMES A. 1994. *Multiethnic Education.* 3d ed. Needham Heights, MA: Allyn and Bacon.

BARNHARDT, LAURA. 1997. "Have Problems? Cheltenham Students Have Solutions." *Philadelphia Inquirer,* 22 June, MC 1–2.

BOAL, AUGUSTO. 1992. *Games for Actors and Non-Actors.* Translated from the French by Adrian Jackson. London: Routledge.

———. 1979. *Theatre of the Oppressed.* New York. Theatre Communications Group.

BOLIN, GAVIN. 1979. *Towards a Theory of Drama in Education.* London: Longman.

COOPERSMITH, JEROME. 1970. *Professional Writers Teleplay/Screenplay Format.* New York: WRITERS GUILD OF AMERICA/EAST, INC.

COURTNEY, RICHARD. 1990. *Drama and Intelligence.* Montreal: McGill-Queen's University Press.

———. 1982. *Re-Play: Studies of Drama in Education.* Toronto: Institute for Studies in Education.

———. 1974. *Play, Drama and Thought.* New York: Drama Book Specialists.

COWLEY, GEOFFREY, and KAREN SPRINGEN. 1995. "Rewriting Life Stories." *Newsweek,* 17 April, 70–74.

DOWNS, WILLIAM, and LOU ANNE WRIGHT. 1998. *Playwriting from Formula to Form.* Orlando, FL: Harcourt Brace & Co.

FELNER, MIRA. 1989. *Free to Act.* New York: Holt, Rinehart & Winston.

FIELD, SYD. 1994. *Screenplay: The Foundations of Screenwriting.* New York: Bantam/Doubleday.

FISHER, ROGER, and WILLIAM URY. 1981. *Getting to Yes, Negotiating Agreement Without Giving In.* Boston: Houghton Mifflin.

FOX, JONATHAN, ed. 1987. *The Essential Moreno.* New York: Springer.

FURMAN, LOU. 1997. "Drama with an At-Risk High School Population: Making a Difference." *Stage of the Art* 9 (3): 13–16.

GARDNER, HOWARD. 1991. *The Unschooled Mind: How Children Think and How Schools Should Teach.* New York: Basic Books.

GOLEMAN, DANIEL. 1995. *Emotional Intelligence.* New York: Bantam Books.

HARRIS, AURAND. 1964. *Androcles and the Lion.* New Orleans: Anchorage Press.

INSTITUTE FOR MENTAL HEALTH INITIATIVE. 1988. *RETHINK! Conflict Management Techniques.* Champaign, IL: Research Press.

JENNINGS, SUE. 1986. *Creative Drama in Groupwork.* London: Winslow Press.

———. 1974. *Remedial Drama.* New York: Theatre Arts.

JONES, PHIL. 1996. *Drama as Therapy: Theatre as Living.* London and New York: Routledge.

JOHNSON, DAVID, and ROBERT JOHNSON. 1995. *Reducing School Violence.* Alexandria, VA: Association for Supervision and Curriculum Development.

LANDY, ROBERT. 1994. *Persona and Performance.* London: Jessica Kingsley.

———. 1986. *Drama Therapy.* Springfield, IL: Chas. C. Thomas.

———. 1982. *Handbook of Educational Drama and Theatre.* New York: Greenwood.

McCASLIN, NELLIE. 1990. *Creative Dramatics in the Classroom and Beyond.* 6th ed. New York: Longman.

MORENO, J. L. 1975. *Psychodrama.* 3d volume. Beacon, NY: Beacon House.

———. 1973. *The Theatre of Spontaneity.* 2d ed. Beacon, NY: Beacon House.

O'NEILL, CECILY, and ALAN LAMBERT. 1990. *Drama Structures.* Portsmouth, NH: Heinemann.

POE, EDGAR ALLAN. 1975. *Complete Tales and Poems.* New York: Vintage Books.

ROSENBLATT, ROGER. 1995. "Teaching Johnny to Be Good." *New York Times,* 30 April, 36–41, 50, 60, 64, 74.

SCOTT, GINI GRAHAM. 1990. *Resolving Conflict with Others and Within Yourself.* Oakland, CA: New Harbinger Publications.

SHAW, G. B. 1962. *Complete Plays with Prefaces.* Vol. 3. New York: Dodd, Mead & Co.

SPOLIN, VIOLA. 1970. *Improvisations for the Theatre.* Evanston, IL: Northwestern University Press.

STANFORD, BARBARA. 1995. "Conflict and the Story of Our Lives: Teaching English for Violence Prevention." *English Journal* (Sept.): 38–42.

STERNBERG, PATRICIA. 1982. *On Stage: How to Put on a Play.* New York: Julian Messner.

———, and DOLLY BEECHMAN. 1989. *SoJourner.* New Orleans: Anchorage Press.

———, and ANTONINA GARCIA. 1989. *Sociodrama: Who's In Your Shoes?* New York: Praeger Publishers.

WAY, BRIAN. 1967. *Development Through Drama.* Atlantic Highlands, NJ: Humanities Press.

WILSON, EDWIN. 1976. *The Theatre Experience.* New York: McGraw Hill.

ZUCCHINO, DAVID. 1995. "Hands-on Efforts Take on Violence at Its Roots." *Philadelphia Inquirer,* 8 May, A1–8.